The Two Sides of Every Dollar

The Hidden Teachings of How Money
Shapes Your Life

MATTHEW MILLER

LUCIDBOOKS

The Two Sides of Every Dollar
The Hidden Teachings of How Money Shapes Your Life
Copyright © 2025 by Matthew Miller

Published by Lucid Books in Houston, TX
www.LucidBooks.com

All rights reserved. No part of this publication may be reproduced, stored in a retrieval system, or transmitted in any form by any means, electronic, mechanical, photocopy, recording, or otherwise, without the prior permission of the publisher, except as provided for by USA copyright law.

Unless otherwise indicated, scripture quotations are taken from the Holy Bible, New Living Translation, copyright ©1996, 2004, 2015 by Tyndale House Foundation. Used by permission of Tyndale House Publishers, Carol Stream, Illinois 60188. All rights reserved.

ISBN: 978-1-63296-869-2
eISBN: 978-1-63296-871-5

Special Sales: Most Lucid Books titles are available in special quantity discounts. Custom imprinting or excerpting can also be done to fit special needs. Contact Lucid Books at Info@LucidBooks.com

The financial concepts and hypothetical examples presented within this book are intended only for educational purposes. This information should not be considered investment advice or a recommendation of any particular security, strategy, or product.

Advisory Persons of Thrivent Advisor Network provide advisory services under a "doing business as" name or may have their own legal business entities. However, advisory services are engaged exclusively through Thrivent Advisor Network, LLC, a registered investment adviser. Awaken Wealth Partners and Thrivent Advisor Network, LLC are not affiliated companies. Information in this message is for the intended recipient[s] only. Please visit our website, www.awakenwealthpartners.com, for important disclosures.

Securities offered through Thrivent Investment Management Inc. ("TIMI"), member FINRA and SIPC, and a subsidiary of Thrivent, the marketing name for Thrivent Financial for Lutherans. Thrivent.com/disclosures. TIMI and Awaken Wealth Partners are not affiliated companies.

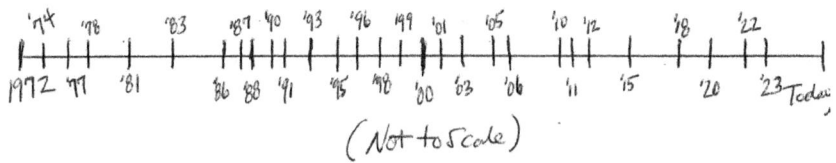

(Not to scale)

During each of these times in my life, and several others between the dates shown, a relationship mattered.

Someone invested in me. Someone chose me. Someone protected me. Someone saved me. Someone sacrificed something for me. Someone said yes. Someone prayed with me or over me. Someone entrusted me with something or someone important to them. Someone accepted me as their own. Someone educated me. Someone disciplined me. Someone provided for me. Someone carried me. And, someone encouraged me.

I am forever thankful to the dozens of people that are a part of my story. I am better because of them. I love you.

me

Table of Contents

Preface	ix
The Why	1
What Do I See?	2
Who?	4
How?	5
Understanding Your Priorities	7
Application	9
Leadership	10
Read the Room	11
Investing	12
Debt	12
Spending	14
Application	15
Generosity	15
Taxes	16
Leadership	17
Wisdom	19
Where Do We Find Wisdom?	19
How Does Wisdom Relate to the Use of Money?	21
Application	24
Measuring the Qualitative Aspects of Life	24
Leadership	28
Wealth, Debt, and Beneficiaries	31
Application	35

Understanding Your Yield Curve	39
Applications	43
Leadership	44
Personal Life	44
Investing	45
Value of Your Time	47
Application	50
Leadership	54
Lifestyle Creep . . .	57
Applications	61
Purpose	67
Application	70
Leadership	71
Fiduciary	73
Application	75
Rule of 72	79
Application	83
Leadership	86
Inflation	87
Application	90
Lifestyle	92
Leadership	92
Four Pillars of Health	93
Valued Relationships	93
Interest	95
Compounding Interest	95
Simple Interest	101
Application	103
Leadership	104

Your Strategy Matters (to Your Money and Your Life)	107
Dollar Cost Averaging	107
Application	110
Application	112
Application	116
Sequence of Returns	121
Application	128
Growth	131
Application	136
Communication	139
Exchange Rates	145
Applications	152
Risk	157
Application	159
Professional Weaknesses	166
Net Worth	173
Application	187
Lines of Credit	191
Benchmarks	199
Giving	201
Saving	201
Spending	202
Debt	203
Taxes	203
Emergency Fund Ratio	204
Credit Score	205
Insurance Benchmarks	205
Return on Investment (ROI) Percentage	205
Seasonality	206

Net Worth	206
Wealth Quotient	206
Bottom line, Profitability, Profit & Loss Statement	206
Closing Thoughts	208
Applications	211
Leadership	212
Let's Land the Plane	213
Visualization	217
Family Meetings	221
Interest-Based	230
Planning	233
Purpose	234
Team	235
Plan	237
So Now What?	251
Acknowledgments	257
Notes	259
About The Author	261

Preface

I believe one of the most impactful catalysts to the trajectory of one's future is the proper use of the imagination and telling one's life story. I dream about families, marriages, individuals, organizations, and businesses seeking a life that is richer and fuller than could ordinarily be expected. Yet, I know that my dear friend Daron said, "We often run at a pace that if we're not careful, we're soon to have a rear end collision with ourselves."

Many great stories, hopes, dreams, and God's plans for us are not realized as often as they could be for many reasons, the primary one being a lack of direction. We have heard many clichés of old, including: "Proper planning prevents poor performance," "He who fails to plan is planning to fail," "A goal without a plan is simply a dream." I'm also reminded of the Scripture that says, "*For where your treasure is, there your heart will be also*" (Matthew 6:21 ESV). Yet, as much as we like to think we are multitasking, it seems we're often more distracted than productive.

There is a tremendous upside available for all who apply themselves. You and I may differ in our beliefs, backgrounds, upbringing, experiences, careers, goals, and many other valued aspects, but we are both human. We are very similar in many ways. So, how do we best equip ourselves to seek the highest possible life trajectory? How do we prepare for the climb, the descent, and the valley floors of life?

I, personally and professionally, believe the answer lies in taking an all-encompassing approach with planning. I know . . . I know . . .

planning is nothing earth-shattering; it is nothing new. It is not new in concept, but maybe it's new to you. It doesn't have to be earth-shattering to be valuable.

The importance of planning has been known for decades, yet most individuals, households, and marriages are not utilizing this best practice. Why is that? After all, let's review the benefits: Planning keeps us focused; it engages the imagination, helps prevent distractions, improves communication, is transferable to the next generation, improves our children's future, promotes learning, strengthens our relationships, and changes lives. And these are just a few of the positives. There is no need to engage in the futile exercise of reviewing the reasons or excuses to avoid planning.

My hope is that this book changes your thoughts on the importance of holistic planning and demonstrates why it is worthwhile to approach planning from a holistic perspective. I pray that the material in this book positively alters the course of every person who reads and implements the strategies we discuss. I also pray that this book sheds light on our potential together as sons and daughters of the one living God.

The Why

The most expensive real estate on the planet is your mind.

Why do I care enough to write this book? In my personal and professional life, I see many individuals, marriages, families, nonprofits, and businesses struggle for many reasons while others thrive in what I refer to as a life lived in abundance. I am writing this book because I care and because people, marriages, and outcomes matter; each person's story is relevant and I care about the future . . . your future . . . my future.

The most expensive real estate on the planet is your mind.

I am not writing this book because I feel I know it all. I don't. Instead, this is the culmination of my life experience and knowledge in written form. Many books that speak about improvement are written as autobiographies, journals, memoirs, or some combination. This book is no different in that regard.

My parents divorced when I was two and, for a few years, it was just my mom and me. Thankfully, she met a man who took on the challenge of raising a family and a son that was not his (biologically). He was also divorced and had two daughters. Growing up in a blended family had its challenges. Fast-forward some twenty-five years later, I followed a similar path. I made my mistakes along the way! I can hear the beep–

beep–beep as the dump truck backs up to haul them off . . . that is, when I allow my mistakes to be hauled off rather than accumulate.

I'm thankful you are reading this book and that we get this opportunity to learn and share time together. For starters, I'd like to lay this ground rule: It is very important that we acknowledge that it is OK not to be perfect. I know . . . I know, we say that all the time, but I'm tired of paying lip service that temporarily comforts us like the room service that keeps us in our room.

It is OK to address the unhealthy things we learned from our parents. It is OK to talk about the things we've done to ourselves and others. It is OK to address the failures, fears, doubts, concerns, guilt, shame, and other issues many of us face. Anyone who tells you otherwise is, unfortunately and most likely, imprisoned by the very things they refuse to discuss.

The simple truth is that I've been there. One of the debt instruments that I learned growing up is pride. I'm not referring to the healthy pride though I learned that later. I'm referring to the kind of pride that tells you to stuff it down, move on, don't talk about it, and keep pushing on—the arrogant type of pride. The type that is said to make you tougher. Unfortunately, that is correct; it will make you tougher. It made me tougher to be around; it made me difficult to work with, be married to, love, and care for.

There, you have it. Come on back . . . beep–beep–beep . . . you can have this trash called pride. I want to live in abundance, not scarcity. Did you notice the phrase *debt instrument* above? We'll touch on that later, but in short, debt comes in various forms.

What Do I See?

In life and work, I often see a scarcity mentality comprised of little to no margin—reserves that are on empty. I see a hurriedness rather than a productiveness, a no endgame in mind approach, and little to no direction. I also see the speed at which we operate, creating unique struggles in our marriages, homes, work environments, communities, and culture. The struggle is real. Yet it is almost foreign to us as if we are streaming our life's story with a remote in hand, rather than paying attention to our own lives.

The perceived problem from my personal and professional experience is that we have a supercomputer mind that sits on our shoulders, and it is gradually being slowed by the shiny quarters or circumstances of life. Like Dug, the talking dog in the movie *UP*, we are moving right along when suddenly we hear, "Squirrel!" And the problem is worsening . . .

It is like running out of storage on our phone; we are slowing our own progress down with clutter. There seems to be a lot of talk about advocacy, but it sure seems like we're not very tolerant of each other. Finally, I think we need to believe once again that each of our stories matters and that no one's story is more important than another. And as our stories are woven together, life thrives.

For many years I struggled to find the best way to launch this writing project while adulting (i.e., trying to be a better dad, loving our daughter, living through a pandemic, running a business, going through a divorce, coping with COVID-19, and changing churches after over thirty years). I have struggled with how to start and build momentum. But unlike essay assignments required in school, life does not have quarters or semesters that end with required assignments. Instead, life has a cruel way of getting faster and harder with no scheduled fall and spring breaks.

Being vulnerable for a moment, as a Christian I struggled with deciding what perspective I should take in writing this book. Thankfully, I recalled something that my grandma's denture story imparted to me: Do not try to be someone you're not. Instead, be genuine and authentic. If I try something on for size, it might look OK aesthetically, but it will not have the authenticity that I aspire to have. We may differ in some respects, but I think most of us value integrity and authenticity.

In the short term, not approaching this writing with all that I am might be more comfortable or more "marketable," but then again who says being comfortable is best. Were those who created industries, inspired change, or bet the farm on a brighter future comfortable? No! Being comfortable with being uncomfortable is more sustainable, and why would any of us permit others to determine *our* comfort level? Think about how many original inspirations and masterpieces the world has missed because of someone's decision to not do something based on what others might think. Or maybe worse, how many things have we all done so we would be liked by others. Much like my grandma's dentures, they may partially fit and look original, but they do not meet the Maker's standards. Interestingly, once I stood firm on my direction, something happened. The writer's block went away. I hope you keep reading.

Who?

It is my goal to share and be vulnerable and transparent as well as to challenge and enlighten us. I hope to inspire intentionality, help boost confidence, promote change, and improve the trajectory of lives. Whose lives, you may ask? Our lives . . . together. Remember, I have my own dump truck of mistakes as well as potential. I'll never be perfect on earth, so this is as much for me as it is for everyone who keeps reading. Let's own our collective messes together, learn how to drive the truck, and navigate through the streets of life together, while aiming for significance.

How?

Over the past thirty years, I have learned that our income and the money we have has a unique way of teaching us many things. For example, Jesus is a well-known part of history and whether we agree on His purpose, His words often reference money, and His purpose was to create a connection. He frequently used parables as teaching tools because stories are relatable and easier to grasp. For example, if I were to say, "Go into your cupboard, pantry, or food closet and pull out all the ingredients to make your favorite dessert," that would make sense. However, not everyone has the ingredients, knowledge, oven, or time to bake their favorite dessert. Some don't have a pantry or even a favorite dessert. The same applies to money and its relation to life, marriage, raising children, career, retirement, and death. Some have dreams, and some can't dream now. Some live in abundance; most don't. In this example, money is equivalent to the ingredients for the dessert; the pantry is the bank, and the investment account and the dessert are the dreams for the future. Money is required throughout our lives, and it should be included in more conversations. All topics, whether macro or micro, have an element that is at a minimum, tethered to money.

So, why is money not discussed more frequently in our homes, businesses, churches or communities? We'll talk more about this question later. For now, let's focus on the how. Money has five uses (5Us), and these uses should be talked about more because many of life's best-kept secrets can be discovered in these 5Us. I also believe this is why I'm here. Part of my life's story or purpose is to talk about these taboo subjects and bring health to individuals, homes, marriages, families, businesses, and communities.

Our routines and habits related to money tell us a lot about ourselves . . . if we will listen. When we observe, accept, and look for brighter tomorrows, we grow. I also know that our own 5Us come with some self-imposed judgment for many. I encourage you to kick that debt instrument thought known as judgment to the curb and exchange it with the wealthy thought of growth. Your money is speaking to you now. Let's listen to what it's telling us.

Understanding Your Priorities

What are the two things you value most? Please don't skim over this question. Knowing what we value most is important for each of us. I value my faith and family above all other things in life.

What about you, what are the two things you value most? Follow-up question: Because you value these two things most, how are you protecting and investing in them?

For health-related goals we measure improvements in distance, speed, reps, sleep, intake, output, weight lifted, and the pounds on a scale. For investing, we look at our accounts and expect to see improvement. For generosity, we strive to accomplish personal goals that we feel mirror our best self. For sports, we count wins and losses. In fact, much of what we do in life can be counted. This is referred to as quantitative. But what about the things we value that aren't as easy to measure? This is referred to as qualitative. How do we measure the quality of what we value most?

For what I value most, how can I measure the quality of my faith journey and my family? In my experience, this is one of the biggest stumbling blocks to effective communication and planning. Not knowing how to effectively do something that we know will be beneficial creates tension within us. And if that tension isn't resolved, we tend to act in unproductive, sometimes, negative ways. Here are a few examples:

- We don't say anything at all.
- We lean on emotions to express a deeper question or concern.
- We increase the volume.
- We walk away.
- We blame others.
- We shut down.

Wait a minute; hold the phone! What does this have to do with money, you may be asking. Answer: From a monetary perspective, money is a necessary and useful resource. What you may not know is that money is also an extremely valuable life learning resource. Money isn't limited to how we can leverage it for a better retirement. It also provides dozens of life lessons that help us build a brighter future. It's in the various combinations of the monetary and personal learning from which every person can benefit.

And this is how we measure the qualitative. We start with a growing awareness of its presence in our lives. We experience effective communication with others and ourselves. We see with wider, more intentional lenses. We're more attentive to our experiences. We listen more intently. Our proximity with others and even ourselves begins to matter more. Logic and emotion cohabitate thought more effectively. And the hundreds of combinations of quality and quantity begin to bear fruit that can be measured with the presence of peace, joy, growth, gratitude, accountability, and so many other fruitful aspects of life. This is why knowing how we're investing, protecting, and planning for what we value most is important to every home, business, and organization.

As an extremely important resource, money is the engine that can produce abundant horsepower for our lives, homes, marriages, businesses, nonprofits, legacies, and communities. And yes, retirement.

Let's consider what money can teach us and how we can leverage this valuable resource; the first step is to answer these questions:

1. What two things do you value most?

- _____
- _____

2. After your top two, what are your tier 2 things you value?

- _____
- _____
- _____

Earlier I mentioned that the two things I value most are faith and family. My tier 2 things I value most are career, friends/social life, and hobbies. What are yours?

Application

Without knowing what we value most, it's hard to create focus, build moats around and invest in what we value. It's also hard to build healthy routines. When we know what we value most, we are more aware of the fact that others also have things they value. For married couples, taking time to know what each other values is a healthy exercise, and this also creates a lot of alignment for planning.

Leadership

It is never safe to assume that our teams value the same things we value or that they desire career trajectories like the trajectory we envision for them. It is wise to remember that no one anywhere can think for anyone else. That is an impossible feat; yet how many "think" they know how others think? A couple of helpful hints here:

- Actions are not guaranteed displays of thought.
- Not everyone dreams.
- Where there is smoke, fire exists; whether smoldering or a blaze, smoke is a telling sign.
- Thought patterns are pliable.

Using the two values questions above will make a difference in how you lead your teams. You have thoughts, struggles, aspirations, failures, and successes, and so does everyone on your team. Watch what transparency does for your team and you. Watch how something that is qualitative translates to productive days. Don't just talk about how high tides raise all ships without trying to build the levees, dams, and bridges to help.

If it's valuable, it's worth measuring.

Read the Room

The thought of "read the room" usually implies some form of empathy or understanding of the group that someone is speaking with or hanging out with. Question: How often do you think about what you're thinking about? How often do you evaluate your routines to see if they are complementing or depreciating what you value most? Do you review your words and actions to discern whether they are investing in what you value or possibly adding debt or taxing situations?

So, with your average day in mind, how do the things you do complement the two things you value most? What about your tier 2 things you value? As you consider these questions, let's talk about the five uses (5Us) of money:

- **Generosity:** When we give cash to someone in need or a gift to an organization to support a cause, we are being generous. We can also be generous with our time and talents.
- **Saving:** When we save money for a rainy day, retirement, college, or big purchases, we are investing in a future season of life.
- **Spending:** When we spend money on food, gas, beverages, phone, vacation, and so on we are spending money on items that are needed or desired.

- **Debt:** When we borrow, we acknowledge that money is being borrowed in exchange for a cost, and we owe that debt plus interest back to the lender.
- **Taxes:** When we own property, earn income, grow assets, and purchase goods, depending upon where we live, we pay various forms of taxes.

Everything we use our hard-earned income toward falls within one of these five uses (5Us). The challenge for us is to understand how the way we use our money and leverage our daily activities complements the things we value most.

Investing

If family is one of the two things you value most, are the things you're doing throughout the week investing in family? Some examples may include time, proximity, active listening, conversation, and activities. To intentionally invest in something throughout the week is to desire an outcome that is brighter years from now. Investing takes on various forms; it's not just about the value of investment accounts.

Debt

Debt is one of the 5Us; the two common forms of debt are a mortgage and credit card debt. Let's apply the same scrutiny to debt as we did for investing. What are the things you do throughout the week that relate to debt? Before you respond, remember that debt in monetary terms is the borrowing of money, most often with interest accruing like a mortgage or compounding like a credit card. We'll talk more about interest in a later chapter.

Here's an example from my life. I'm not good at sitting idle. I really enjoy what I do for a living. I have a love, hate, then love again relationship with golf. I'm competitive. And being authentic,

I enjoy a cold one on the hot summer days and good bourbon. And that's just off the top of my head. Neither of these is bad, wrong, or related to debt. In fact, in many ways they can complement each other. That is until I choose to partake in either one of these in an unhealthy way and permit these, tier 2 or tier 3 things, to overtake the top position.

Sorry, Mom, I know you dislike that I said I like beer. But the thought of continuing to promote an unauthentic life exhausts me. In fact, it's not the golf, work, home, stuff, food, or drink, it's the people that I get the privilege of knowing and sharing life with that I enjoy the most.

Seasons of struggle exist, and there will be seasons when the workload is heavy. But seasons run their course; that's to be expected. But when winter lasts twelve months, something has gone wrong, and if the situation is not addressed, some form of debt builds up in our lives. Enough about the debt I strive to eliminate, what about you?

Let's keep the focus on mortgage and credit card examples for now. A mortgage is sometimes referred to as a "good" debt, whereas owing on credit cards is not. So, we work to pay down good debt and provide a roof over our family's heads and provide security. Conversely, using a credit card to inflate our income and then owing interest is not a best practice.

Metaphorically, have you ever thought about how much debt we're costing ourselves with procrastination, negative self-talk, and routines that don't invest in the things we value most? The interest that accrues or compounds because of these behaviors takes on various forms and is costly when not addressed. Think about it for a minute. When borrowed money is not paid back, there are negative impacts such as a lower credit score and, in some instances, repossession of goods purchased on credit.

Here are some of the forms of non-monetary interest that can affect us personally: poor health, angst, lack of sleep, regret, and distance in valued relationships. These affect us negatively and much like monetary interest on debt, they have compounding effects.

Spending

By volume, the most frequent use of money is spending. No matter the household income, this is the category where most of our income is used; it includes the money that we spend on the items we need and enjoy. In my profession, the money we spend on items we enjoy is often referred to as discretionary income; that is, money available after basic needs have been met.

Here's an interesting perspective on our spending in relation to the other 5Us. For the most part, our spending is for consumption as we purchase basic needs and spend money on the things we enjoy. For example, when I pay for a round of golf and eat and have a drink afterward, I hopefully enjoy the round. Which can be an investment in my physical, emotional, and mental health, but the money spent on all three is never to return. Our groceries are a requirement and hopefully an investment in our physical health, but again, that amount is never to return. And what we consume is literally dispensed as waste.

Consumption is required, and there is no argument or judgment to the contrary. My point is simply that much of what we do daily and most of what we spend our hard-earned income on is gone in a short time, never to return. We might say that vacations, experiences, health memberships, and the like are exceptions in that these build fond memories and invest in the four pillars of our spiritual, mental, emotional, and physical health. This is an example of the two sides of every dollar: One side is never to return; yet the other side is investing in quality of life.

But for the most part, what we spend has a burn rate. What part of your week goes toward your needs as part of the needed consumption, enjoyment, and waste equation? Sleep, our thoughts, our screen time, our creature comforts—how much of our days is spent bringing value, being consumed, and being wasted?

Application

I'm going to drop our first **Wealth Coordinate** (WC) here. A WC is a thought, action, routine, or some combination of the three that is pivotal to our individual and collective success. In some instances, it's like a coordinate on a map that locates a position; in other instances, it's like a pin that is dropped by someone else so we can find a place we're looking for. Our first Wealth Coordinate is a combo.

You may be familiar with the quote from Jim Rohn that says, "You are the average of the five people you surround yourself with."[1] Here's the **Wealth Coordinate**: Our 5Us can be our best friends and they can help any one of us reach the highest mountaintops, personally, professionally, and monetarily. But much like one friend can spoil the friend circle, so can the use known as spending. It is the highest percentage of most household incomes, and we know what happens to a percentage when one input is higher than the others. I encourage you to remember that consumption is often transactional, and from a monetary perspective, that's acceptable and understood. However, our values, quality of life, and the things we treasure personally aren't transactional. Let's not allow the transactional aspect of money to overshadow what we value most.

Generosity

When cash is given to an organization to support a cause or given to an individual, you're being generous or as some say, you're paying it forward or bringing it back. Either way this is generosity. This 5U is really important to our personal lives. During the week, how generous are you to yourself in the form of kindness, forgiveness, and grace? From a monetary perspective, some say that if it can't be given, then who owns who? Interestingly, if we're not generous to or forgiving ourselves, are we likely to share these attributes with others? For some, the answer is yes; these are the very rare, dearly beloved people who sacrifice all of themselves for others. However, this approach can come with the debt of not investing in themselves.

Taxes

The last of the 5Us is taxes. As referenced earlier, when money is earned, invested, or spent, a portion will go toward various forms of taxes. Here in the US, our taxes are federal, state, and local; tax rates vary by income, filing status, possessions, and state. When translated to our personal life, taxes sometimes overlap with debt metaphorically. I liken it to our self-worth, productivity, and similar attributes. For example, I know that what I earn is going to be taxed according to the government entities just mentioned. Therefore, my net income after taxes is what goes toward the other four uses of the money I earn. Personally, when I'm not investing or being generous to myself or others, I may limit my potential by taxing margin or space. For example, if I don't know how to say no, I say yes. Therefore, my margin for time is less, which depletes my earning potential personally.

Here's why knowing how to leverage these 5Us is helpful to many of the most successful people and businesses. Most of our daily activities fall within one of these 5Us. From a good night's sleep to constructive feedback, how we invest in ourselves and others matters. In being generous with our time, such as having an open-door policy at work or having an abundance mentality in sharing best practices, we open doors. From a spending perspective, we know that how we spend our waking and sleeping hours matters. From a debt perspective, some debt is better than others, but we also need to keep a close watch on what kinds of debt we permit emotionally and mentally. From a monetary perspective, we know that taxes must be paid, but must we tax ourselves and others, emotionally and mentally as much as we do?

You and the spheres you influence will benefit from a working knowledge of your 5Us, personally, professionally, and monetarily.

Leadership

You should know and discuss the 5Us for your organization and your teams; the discussion can be held openly and during individual conversations. For example, you know your objectives and what resources are available to put toward those.

For example, you know the work objectives, key performance indicators (KPIs), and company resources available to meet annual goals. You also know that the best part of every organization is the people. So, have you, as a leader, invested in others and assessed whether thoughts, words, and actions of your team are more investment-oriented than not? The same goes for the daily routines of your team. If you often wonder about mission loss or team culture, it would be helpful to know what is being filed mentally as a taxing or debt-laden thought.

Here's another useful question to consider: How generous is the team with each other's time and sharing of best practices and career paths? If the team isn't rowing together, then there will be slack.

Homes, offices, and communities that work toward a common good frequently exhibit positive characteristics such as greener pastures, upward and to the right results, and calm during a storm. More often than not, favorable characteristics aren't simply stumbled upon; rather they must be cultivated.

Wisdom

"If you had to choose a bag of gold or a tablet carved with words of wisdom, which would you choose?" This challenging question is from the book *The Richest Man in Babylon*.[2] If you haven't read this classic, I recommend that you pick up a copy.

Where Do We Find Wisdom?

Wisdom is available to all who seek, listen, and invest in themselves. Wisdom is less elusive than many think. It can be found, learned, stored, applied, given, repeated, misinterpreted, and passed by. It exists abundantly among us as we wake, work, play, and sleep. The question then is, "Where do I find wisdom?

Answer: Wisdom is gleaned from others and from our experiences. It is like energy; it can change from one form to another without being lost. Let's think for a moment about how you might have gleaned wisdom from others. Did you have grandparents who invested in your upbringing? If so, they likely shared wisdom with you. What about your parents? Wisdom is often passed down from one generation to the next. Unfortunately, though, not everyone had parents or grandparents who invested in them while they were growing up.

Wisdom may also be gleaned from people closest to us—our advocates. Who do you confide in? Do you have a team of professionals who speak into your life? If so, wisdom is what you're paying for. Valued relationships that go beyond the client or professional level are often a wonderful source of wisdom. Not only do we need others to invest their wisdom in us, but we also need to invest wisdom in others. Wisdom thrives in this environment. Have you experienced the phenomenon of how much you learn while teaching someone else? Wisdom shared is wisdom multiplied.

How are you investing in yourself via what you are reading, watching, listening, and participating in? All these activities and interactions can be valuable sources of wisdom. And for many, wisdom is gleaned from a higher being. For perspective, the Christian believes wisdom comes from God. In fact, James 1:5 says, *"If you need wisdom, ask our generous God, and he will give it to you. He will not rebuke you for asking."*

One of the keys to applying wisdom well is to recognize that life is not a do-it-yourself (DIY) project. We need others investing in us as we attend to our lives. The thought of being able to live this life abundantly without the assistance of others is a self-fulfilling prophecy. The more of self you seek, the more of self you will receive. All the while, edging out others who could ultimately make us better as we grow lonelier.

Several paths of wisdom can be gleaned from how we invest in our spiritual, mental, emotional, and physical health (sometimes referred to as the "Four Pillars"). For example, most of us understand that to be human is to be selfish. So, on a continuum for selfishness, where do you suspect you live? Do you serve yourself more than others or serve both equally or serve others to your own detriment? From the answers to these questions, we can learn a lot about ourselves, and the byproduct is more wisdom. For example, we might learn that, over time, we are becoming less absorbed in ourselves and more investment-oriented in the lives of others. As the continuum develops, the byproduct is more wisdom. Who wins in this, you ask? Answer = 2 > 1.

As mentioned earlier, wisdom can be gleaned from our experiences, some of which may be less than pleasant. For good or bad, wisdom is often discovered on the valley floors of life—in our rock-bottom trials, which tend to promote focus. Although we love celebrating the mountaintop experiences, rarely do we stop to journal what, how, and who made them happen. We love talking about "the why"; although that is important, let's not forget the other noteworthy aspects of our peak experiences.

How Does Wisdom Relate to the Use of Money?

So how does wisdom affect our behavior associated with money? To answer that question, let's probe a little deeper into our attitudes about money. Invest in yourself by taking time to answer the following questions. You will gain wisdom from thinking deeply about your answers and using this process. I promise you will learn something that is applicable to your life as we work through this section:

1. What is your first memory of money?
2. What did your upbringing teach you about money?

Here are my answers to these questions:
- I have very few early memories of money. I remember living in an apartment in downtown Houston with my mom. I remember that she took me to see *Star Wars* when it first came out; it was a rainy day and a little chilly, but it was glorious. On another occasion I remember eating so much spaghetti that I got sick to my stomach. Less glorious but it

was great until it wasn't. Later I learned that my mom earned less than $900 per month. I also remember that my grandma on my mother's side would hide money in coffee cans.

- Years later, after my mom remarried, my upbringing taught me that money is earned from hard work as my parents would leave the house around 5:30 a.m. to be at the office by 6:15 a.m. I also learned that I could earn money by doing chores. The money was paid after chores were completed or not paid if chores weren't done. In my teens, I learned that money provides for our needs; it can be given and saved. We didn't talk about money much, but its purposes were clearly demonstrated.

Here's why your answers matter. Whether we accept this or not, our behaviors associated with money have an origin—often stemming from our earliest training and life experiences. This also applies to many other areas of life including our parenting techniques, traditions, lifestyle, beliefs, eating patterns, spending patterns, and saving patterns. Some of what we learned from our family of origin is beneficial; some behaviors may not be so helpful. Because no one is perfect, it's improbable that we only learned good things from our parents.

Here's my intent in sharing this. To improve or solve anything in life requires knowing the root cause first. Then you can begin to explore solutions from there. To live this life with superficial thinking such as "don't do this or do that" without understanding why doesn't create a sustainable pattern, and it tends to create a judgmental atmosphere. Knowing why we think the way we do, loving ourselves, learning from others, and making healthy changes are more sustainable patterns. My intent is to help narrow the gap with a mind hack process that has worked well for me.

If you didn't answer the previous questions, please do. If you don't want to answer them now, then jot down how you feel and come back to the questions later. How you feel is just as important, and it says something you need to hear. Listen to it.

If you answered the previous questions, what did you learn?

- Did you gain insight into why you have certain patterns (some you like; some you dislike) in your life?
- Did you experience a visceral feeling when you recalled early memories related to money?
- What emotions did your answers evoke?

Your upbringing, emotions, experiences, beliefs, circumstances, dreams, fears, and hopes compete for your attention in deciding what matters most in your life. The same is true for all of us, and these competing forces fight vigorously for our interests, marriages, children, parents, friends, communities, purpose, and passions. For the most part, each area of our lives requires the valuable resource known as money. And our income determines how much we can allocate toward the 5Us introduced in the previous chapter: giving, saving, spending, debt, and taxes.

Let's take the next step (tier 2) in exploring your earliest thoughts about money. Given what you discovered about your earliest memories, answer these questions:

- What is your belief about money?
- How was your belief derived?
- What does your support system or belief system say about money?

Here are my answers to these questions:

- I believe that money helps support our plans, efforts, and dreams. I also know the allure of money can crush the same. My belief is derived from witnessing abundance and scarcity mentalities and the outcomes of each.

- My belief system speaks to generosity, saving, spending, debt, and taxes and the stewardship of each. I believe that by stewarding well, my life and the lives of others can prosper; as stewardship grows, more is given.
- My belief system does not support a prosperity message that implies riches are given for good works.

Application

In life, we often approach a helpful intersection between knowledge and application, both of which are important for our well-being. Knowledge is said to be power. I don't want to toy around with semantics; however, knowledge is simply data and if it is left on the shelf of life, that's not power. In my opinion that would be like approaching the intersection of knowledge and application and taking a detour or U-turn. Instead, knowledge becomes powerful, either good or bad, when it is effectively coupled with application. Gasoline that is put into a container and stored on a shelf has potential, but its complexity begins to diminish over time. However, when gasoline is mixed with air and a spark along with compression, that's when the explosion of horsepower is generated in an engine. A similar process happens in our minds. At the intersection of knowledge and application, life begins to take on new and higher altitudes.

Side note: Gasoline that is stored improperly is extremely dangerous, corrosive, toxic, and potentially deadly. Is there a parallel to knowledge that is not applied? Maybe . . .

Thanks for this, Mike. I value the wisdom gleaned from our intersection conversation we shared years ago.

Measuring the Qualitative Aspects of Life

So how do we measure the qualitative aspects of life that we value most? Let's start by reviewing our answers to questions like the ones you have answered thus far. Your answers provide a basis for having honest and healthy conversations. Recall your answers from earlier in this chapter and the previous one:

- Your answer: I value _____ and _____ above all things.
- Your answer: Earliest memories (review your list).
  Do your earliest memories support what you value most?
    » If yes, how do you further invest in this and support growth?
    » If not, is it time to "sell" these depreciating thoughts and invest in something better?
- Your answer: What your upbringing taught you about money. Did what you learned about money in your childhood support what you value most?
    » If yes, how do you use this to support what you value most and invest in others and yourself?
    » If not, is it time to release these debt instruments and invest in a different line of thought?

If you learned things you'd do differently, jot those down, and we'll map out a path that helps bring value to you and others later. Here are some positive outcomes that can flow out of this exercise:

- Healthier relationships with yourself and others you value most
- Increased communication skills
- Stronger marriage
- Closer relationship with children
- Better professional
- Improved community leader
- A healthier relationship with your 5Us

Is it fair to say that wisdom, for the most part, is helpful? If your answer is yes, then why do you think we do not consistently apply wisdom in our lives? Is it the lack of availability? Nope. For the most part, wisdom is not limited in availability. Is it a lack of know-how? Probably not. Learning how to apply wisdom that betters our lives requires that we first glean it, then understand it, and then apply it. Does wisdom come with age? Yes. Life has a way of teaching us lessons that result in wisdom through our experiences. But remember, age is not an indication of maturity.

What is the answer then? Maybe the search marks the start of your wisdom journey. Here's what I know. I have the privilege of knowing and working with some very intelligent and successful people who have similar traits; they exhibit a thirst for knowledge, a quest for understanding, humility, problem-solving skills, and a desire to learn how to apply wisdom in the best manner possible. I have also gleaned these wisdom nuggets along my journey:

- To earn is to learn.
- To provide is to apply.
- To love is to be loved.
- To forgive is to be forgiven.

Like energy, wisdom lives in a continuous loop, allowing us to serve many at once as readily as we serve another one-on-one.

Have you thought about setting a wisdom goal? While many read, stream, or watch TV for entertainment, others read, watch podcasts, attend seminars, and so on to increase their knowledge, wisdom, and understanding of things.

Quick Mind Hack: Knowledge and wisdom are not the same. Think of knowledge as knowing how to do something. Wisdom is the application. So how are you gleaning and learning more of both? Give these strategies a try. There is a reason why journaling works. There is a reason why writing down your plans is far more productive than only thinking about them. There is a reason why surrounding ourselves with others who have more experience, knowledge, and wisdom is productive. There is a reason why writing and reviewing our goals matters.

A word of caution regarding learning. Retention is great but be sure to guard against an unbalanced ratio of learning and application. It's one thing to have knowledge; yet as we just discussed, it's a completely different thing to see knowledge applied. After all, many of us have met people who speak as if they know everything, yet they have little to no experience. Many years ago, I had a fun conversation with a lady that I often see on the driving range. While we talked shop, we watched one struggling golfer teach another and she said to me, "Isn't interesting how everyone's an instructor now days?" She then proceeded to stripe a drive down the middle of the fairway without saying a word to anyone. I might add that no one asked her questions either. She demonstrated the application of knowledge, whereas the other two talked about knowledge and continued to exhibit poor results. Which result do you seek?

Know where you get your knowledge from. Know the experience level of the person sharing. Hobbies are great to have and it's good to share what we know, but professionals provide a different level of helpful information.

Hopefully, we can agree that we are all uniquely different; yet we have a lot in common. Hopefully, we can also agree that everyone makes mistakes and that none of us will live in perfection. To live a "no-regerts" life is to understand the beauty in that juxtaposition. The person we hold back the most in this life is ourselves. We will have failures; I promise you that you will if you haven't already. We will do things that we hate and wish we could take back. We will say and think things that we hope no one else knows. And everyone you know will do the same—sometimes to us.

Everyone on the planet has to juggle these issues throughout life. To help ourselves with these matters first is to see the beauty in the struggle and then to understand that others face the same struggles. The goal is no regrets but spelled correctly. What a juxtaposition. Love it!

Leadership

Where are you seeking wisdom, and how are you encouraging those around you to see, seek, and experience it? Our responsibility as leaders doesn't start with the transactional aspects that are counted and measured on spreadsheets. Attributes such as genuineness, authenticity, empathy, and the like will yield far more results than attention-grabbing actions that tend to alienate rather than attract.

Wealth Coordinate: Strength under control is an honorable trait called meekness; to be meek is by no means weak.

Our personal growth, much like our finances, may have hints of comparison, judgments, and scarcity, but these are not required. We need not compare ourselves to anyone else on either side of the coin, heads or tails. We know that trying to "fit in" by keeping up with another household's spending can create issues (tails), and we also know that thinking less of ourselves for not being like someone else (heads), is also detrimental. I assure you that, as we engage our frontal lobe more frequently, we will make drastic advancements in our four pillars of health (4Ps) and in our personal and professional lives.

I'm thankful for all the wisdom shared with me and for all those who invested in my life. I am grateful for their prayers, conversations, truth in love discussions, rebukes, debates, encouragement, support, counseling, connections, letters, texts, phone calls, proximity, and time. Each has helped mold, inform, educate, encourage, and hold me accountable.

As you continue your wisdom journey, choose your scouts wisely. Those you allow in your inner circle will take on one or more of the 5U attributes. For example, they will be generous and invest in you, helping build a brighter future. Or they will be detrimental (play on words for debt), taxing and costly, not caring about your future and wasting your time. Sometimes, you may find it difficult to decipher which role they are playing. But when we pay closer attention, you'll see that it gets easier to decipher the fisherman from the one who just tells stories.

Wisdom can be found in many sources, and I encourage you to do your due diligence. Find out which sources are the most reliable and consistent. Know who is your most reliable truth and love provider. Know who is promoting health in your story and not trying to graft their story into yours. And finally, remember there are two sides to every dollar and spending is transactional in nature. Whether purchased online or in a store, most goods will depreciate the minute the exchange of money occurs. Conversely, your life, your 4Ps, your most valued relationships, your career, and your value are generational, and their worth is immeasurable.

So, which is it? Would you prefer a bag of gold or a tablet carved with words of wisdom?

Wealth, Debt, and Beneficiaries

Wealth comes in a variety of forms, as does debt, and both have beneficiaries.

In affluent cultures the word *wealth* typically refers to monetary riches and money in numerical form. Instead, I argue that wealth comes in many forms and that we can be wealthy on many levels, some of which cannot be quantified or accounted for numerically. For example, the wealth we possess includes life, family, marriage, children, health, knowledge, physical attributes, career, friends, education, hobbies, community, and depending upon your spiritual life, a relationship with a higher power. And yes, another example of wealth is money. We will talk more about various aspects of wealth later.

No pun intended, but let's talk about the other side of the coin, debt, which also comes in a variety of forms. Debt is not limited solely to the amount one owes another as a result of borrowing money. Like wealth, debt comes in a variety of forms and takes on an array of characteristics that affect the quality of our lives. From a non-monetary perspective, any number of debt instruments may manipulate their way into our lives; some of these include jealousy, self-doubt, fear, hatred, anxious thoughts, envy, anger, bitterness, unforgiveness, pride, and arrogance. Many of these debt instruments stem from past hurts, our upbringing, circumstances, or consequences that come out of past decisions or outcomes from things beyond our control. And much like wealth, debt also has a monetary component.

However, most people agree that the essence of true wealth comes from what we value most, not purely a numerical value. To prove this assertion, I would simply ask: What did you miss the most when you were quarantined during the COVID-19 pandemic? What did you enjoy the most when communities and cities reopened? Your answers say something about what you value most, which reflects how you measure your wealth.

During the pandemic, I missed being around the people I value. And when communities and cities reopened, I enjoyed interacting with the people who mean the most to me, spending time with others, and being outdoors. So, obviously, my sense of true wealth is tied to the values I shared earlier.

The various forms of debt in our lives (or around us) can rob us of the wealth attributes cited above, much like interest on a loan delays true ownership. For example, sleep robbers such as guilt, shame, fear, and anger can prevent us from getting the seven to eight hours of sleep recommended for a healthy lifestyle. Poor decisions rob us of healthy relationships; arrogance can limit the success we attain in our community or career. The list of "debts" and their side effects ("interest") is limitless, and debts have a propensity to accumulate as fast as high interest accumulates on credit cards, if not faster. But you can't transfer the interest over to a different 0 percent card in real life.

Our wealth and debt affect others because both have beneficiaries. A beneficiary is someone or a legal entity listed to receive the proceeds from an account, such as an investment account or life insurance policy, upon the death of the account owner. For example, a husband or wife who owns an investment account often lists their spouse as the first beneficiary and their children as the contingent beneficiaries. Think of beneficiaries as either first (primary) or second (contingent). In the case of a married couple, when the account owner passes away, the account balance would go to the spouse because of the primary beneficiary designation.

Conversely, when they both pass away, the children become the beneficiaries, and they would receive the account balance upon the death of their parents.

When you hear the word *beneficiary*, think benefit. As the beneficiary of something, you have the potential to benefit from someone's gift (wealth). The beneficiary process occurs at the death of the account owner; yet I humbly submit that although accounts are transferable at death, our wealth attributes and debt characteristics also carry living beneficiaries. That is, while we are alive, we inherit and give things to others, and most often, the beneficiary starts with us!

Allow me to explain with an example. Do you know someone who sees life through a glass half full perspective? What about someone who chooses to see the world through a glass half empty point of view? Do you know someone who is encouraging? Do you know someone who thinks their spiritual gift is criticism? Notice how the characteristics reflect a person's positive or negative point of view:

Glass Half Full	**Glass Half Empty**
Abundance Mentality	Scarcity Mentality
Encouraging	Critiques regularly
Complimentary	Often complains

Consider which perspective—abundance mentality or scarcity mentality—leads to the best benefits for all beneficiaries including oneself, spouse, children, family, neighbors, coworkers, friends, and community? I believe that most of us would prefer to work alongside someone who is productive and who also promotes us and our work (abundance) rather than someone who steps on everyone else to accomplish their own goals (scarcity). I also think we all appreciate seeing our children being encouraged and applauded for accomplishments (abundance) rather than consistently criticized (scarcity). So, abundance wins over scarcity most of the time.

It is important to understand what money is and what it is not. Money is a valuable resource that we earn, receive, or inherit. It allows us to be generous, live life, consume, invest in others, and invest in our future; money is a valuable resource and a form of wealth. However, money is not a living entity. Money is often spoken of as if it is a character in a story as in the popular saying, "Money is one of the top three reasons for divorce." In truth, money is not a living or breathing creation, and it does not have this authority. Remember, it is a valuable resource like clean water, healthy food, and sustainable energy; it is not a person, a living being, or character in our journey.

Money was created as an exchange mechanism and as a valuable resource; it shouldn't create issues in our lives. Instead, valuable resources should bring health, value, and other forms of wealth to our lives. You do not hear people saying that clean water instigates poor health. Instead, the opposite is true: Clean water improves health and life in communities.

Statements such as, "money is one of the top three reasons for divorce" can be classified as a debt instrument, and we should address matters like these head-on. While statements like these may be intended for good, unhealthy habits and behaviors pertaining to money such as the lack of communication, poor decisions, hidden spending, and poor direction can lead to a strained marriage, which then creates separation.

Fallout from actions such as these are often the reasons why marriages, business partnerships, and other valued relationships end in divorce. The reason why money gets a bad rap is that it is easier to blame money than to take ownership of debt instruments such as poor communication, poor habits and behaviors, lack of direction, poor planning, and poor decisions.

Again, money is a very valuable resource, and it's also important to note that money is not a renewable resource. It's earned as we work. It's given when we choose to be generous. It's invested for future use. It's responsibly gathered to collaboratively invest in communities. It's spent as we live. Understanding this cycle means truly accepting the adage: "Money doesn't grow on trees."

Application

Wealth Coordinate: Knowing what we value most and understanding that our wealth attributes complement but our debt instruments negate what we value, is wisdom. To say one thing and do another is no easier to accept than when adults said to us when we were children, "Do as I say, not as I do."

For many reasons, conversations regarding one of the most valuable resources on earth have become taboo, strained, or toxic. In homes, churches, communities, and businesses, various aspects of wealth, such as spending, reserves, profit, work, and other basics have been relegated to a place of insignificance. As a result, people suffer from a lack of knowledge and wisdom.

Most of us would agree that it is more difficult to earn, give, save, spend, and pay taxes than it is to earn, spend, and accumulate debt. For this reason, it is important to understand our own patterns and how they are either benefiting or hurting what we value

> *Most of us would agree that it is more difficult to earn, give, save, spend, and pay taxes than it is to earn, spend, and accumulate debt.*

most. Remember that these comments do not come from a place of comparison or judgment; the purpose of this discussion is to help and grow. There is no need to either gloat about our behavior or demean ourselves; both are debt instruments.

Instead, we need to communicate. I encourage you to be accepting, both as a recipient of someone else's knowledge and your own. Such an attitude is a form of wealth. As general rule, if you fear something, identify it. If you fear public speaking, for example, you can avoid it, and it may or may not hurt your career trajectory. However, if you dislike conversations about money but one of your most valued things is family, then it would be helpful to talk with a trusted professional about the correlation. Why? Because the relation between income and your family's 5Us is important to the mental, emotional, physical, financial, and spiritual health of the very thing you value most (in this example, your family).

In these conversations, meet your spouse, business partner, nonprofit leader, or community leader where they are. That is, seek to understand first rather than seeking to be understood. Learn about their first experiences with money. Ask questions that convey empathy while accepting that most journeys require guides. Accept that no one you know, including yourself, is perfect.

1. What are your various forms of wealth?

2. What are your various forms of debt?

3. Who are the beneficiaries of each?

4. How are your wealth attributes and debt instruments contributing to or diminishing the tier 1 and tier 2 things you value most?

Understanding Your Yield Curve

In my profession and yours, some topics are more difficult to describe than others and, in my world, yield curve is one of them. It is, however, pivotal for our time together and a fundamental concept in the investment world. Hence, we're going to kick off our overview of a series of key investment concepts with a fairly robust discussion of yield curve.

As we know, time is a key component of all aspects of life. Without it, well, our time is up. Another key component to investing and life is interest. Without it, growth in accounts and life slows down or is lost. Let's see how both time and interest play a role in producing yield. What, you may ask, is *yield*? From a production lens, a rancher or farmer will likely define *yield* by saying that the land yields (provides) something that is consumed or sold. A volunteer at a school's crosswalk will likely see *yield* as yielding the right of way to help others pass safely. In investing, yield is income received from investments much like the land yields crops. I submit that all three meanings are applicable to assessing the returns on our lives and accounts.

To help conceptualize the term *yield curve*, let's start with a common definition of interest; that is, interest is the cost to borrow money or profits earned on an investment. In short, the yield curve plots the cost variance over different time periods. Here's a visualization from January 4, 2016, that shows the US Treasuries Yield Curve at different timeframes, from one month to thirty years:

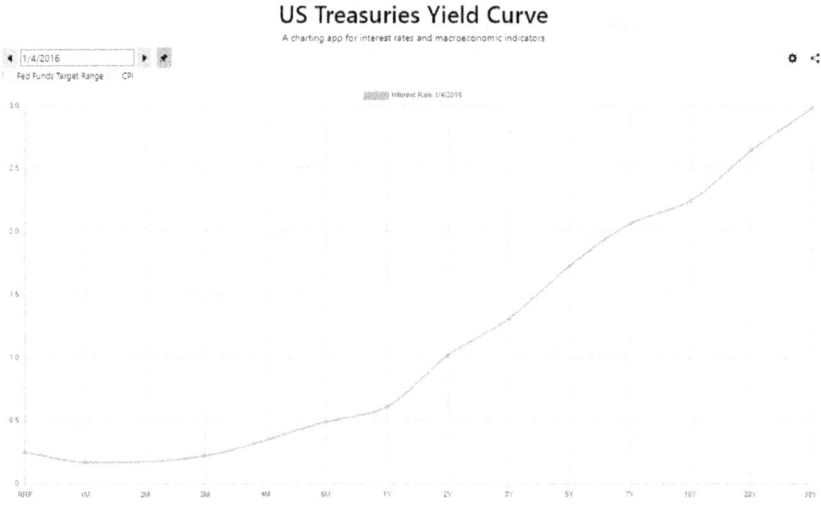

From the graph, we see that on January 4, 2016, the one-year US Treasury would have yielded 0.61%, the two-year 1.02%, and the ten-year 2.24%. This is what is referred to as a "normal" yield curve, which means that short-term yields are lower than long-term yields. This curve is often associated with economic growth and expansion; hence, it's given the "normal" tagline. This makes sense, right? The longer you're employed, the higher your earnings; the longer your money is invested, the higher the account value should be, and here, the longer the money is held, the more interest one should be paid. You've probably heard it said, "You get out what you put in" and "To make money you have to spend money." For growth, lending, and life, the "normal" yield curve is the most desirable of yield curves.

UNDERSTANDING YOUR YIELD CURVE

To contrast this with an inverted yield curve, let's look at yield on the same date but seven years later. The bottom line is the same as above; the top line shows the US Treasuries Yield Curve on January 4, 2023:

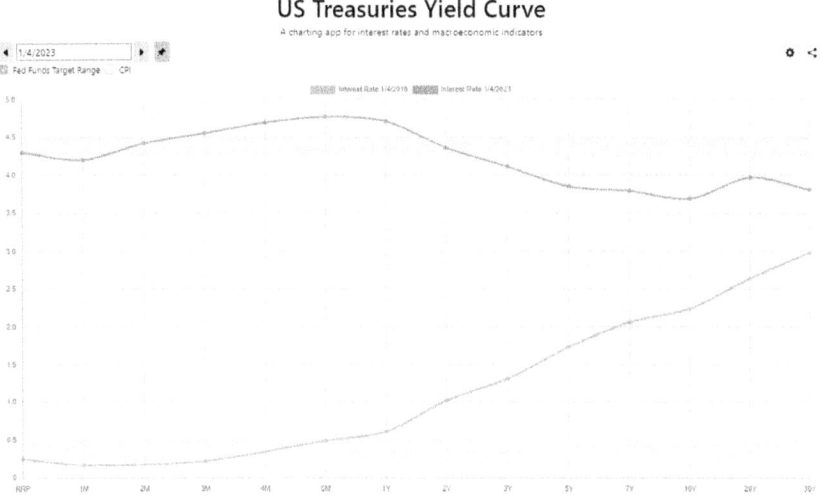

A lot happened in those seven years. First, notice how different the percentages are with the same timeframes. In early 2023 the one-year treasury would have yielded 4.71%; the two-year treasury, 4.36%; and the ten-year treasury, 3.69%. That's quite a change in yield percentages from the previous chart. Also, note the downward trend. This is known as an inverted yield curve because the short-term yield is higher than the long-term yield.

Note that the shaded area near the bottom shows the Fed Funds Rate in early 2016, and the shaded area near the top shows the Fed Funds Rate in early 2023. The Fed Funds Rate is an interest range established by the Federal Reserve, and it's the overnight cost for banks to borrow money, aka the interest rate.

The inverted yield curve shown in the second chart is most often associated with times of economic contraction, or slowing of the economy; it is also considered to be a warning indicator of impending recession.

The third yield curve scenario shown below is known as a flat curve and, as you can imagine, it's when rates are relatively flat for longer periods of time. The graph below is a visual from the early 1980s when interest rates skyrocketed. For many, this was a difficult time as mortgage rates and inflation were insanely high. For comparison, inflation for each year between 1979 and 1981 was higher than it was in 2022. I digress; we'll talk more about inflation in a later chapter.

Here's a visual of a flat rate curve:

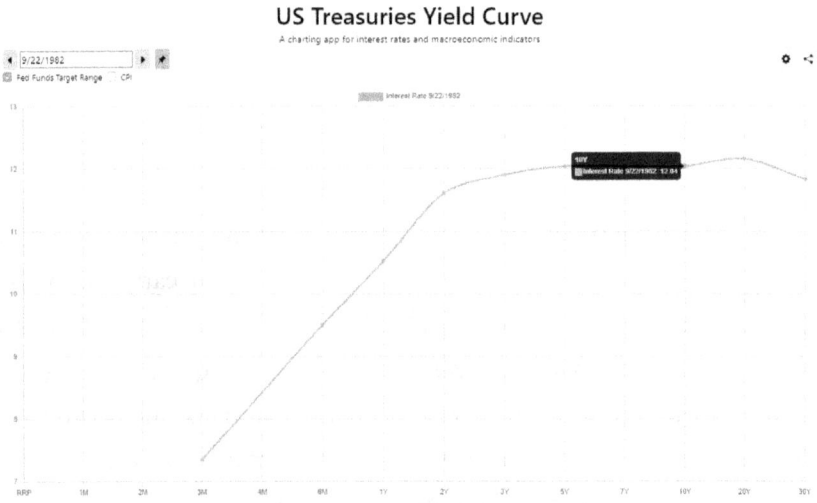

You may have noticed that this flat rate curve is also inverted . . . good catch. Flat rate curves are associated with uncertainty in the economy, a teetering of sorts as the micro and macroeconomics work themselves out.

I know that's a lot of information to digest, but we can take many key concepts from these visuals. We need a working knowledge of yield curves to understand our investment accounts for several reasons:

- Note the interest rate on the flat rate curve. The y-axis starts at 7%, and the one-year yield was north of 10%. That's a healthy return for no market risk, and portfolio managers would help relate that to their clients. This type of higher interest rate environment is helpful for investing but difficult for borrowing.
- Contrast this with the 2016 numbers when interest rates were considerably lower and the yield curve illustrated a healthy economy. This too is helpful knowledge for portfolio construction and for clients to discuss with their wealth managers as portfolio construction should change over time.
- In a world that has added fear and noise as two attention-grabbers, data is useful for drowning out the fearmongers. For example, yes, we did experience an inverted yield curve in 2023, but it's not the yield curve that dictates whether the economy experiences a recession. In fact, there was only one quarter of negative gross domestic product (GDP) from 2020 to 2023, but the sellers of fear and noise were salivating at the thought of the soundbites that followed.

Applications

Wealth Coordinate: Our individual productivity, results, emotions, health, relationships, and everything else in our life will look like one of these charts at some point. Knowing and accepting this is not only healthy, but it is also a linchpin to our success in life.

Leadership

What's the health of your team(s), and how does that correlate with your business results? How are the results trending, and what is the data showing? How does chasing short-term gains forfeit culture and create an inverted yield curve? Productivity, turnover, revenue, morale, profits, and mission are leadership responsibilities, and results in those areas are as much as an indicator of a potential "recession" in the organization's profits as an inverted yield curve is for the US economy.

Your KPIs and the gains related to them can be tracked just as easily as yield. In fact, it's yield of some sort that you're seeking. Be creative and use the y-axis as percentage of accomplishment of KPIs and track the potential yield. Share the results of a "normal," inverted, and flat curve and why they matter over the next several years.

Personal Life

Which yield curve most resonates with your personal life right now? Do you feel like you're trending up or down, or do you feel flat? It is frequently said that seasons come and go, but contrary to this common phrase, the reality is they don't just go. In fact, it takes effort to keep the trend tracking upward and to the right. It takes effort to change the flat feelings of being in a rut. And, yes, the inverted curve happens, but knowing and trusting that you can make a change is essentially your personal "gross domestic product" weapon. Remember that you are the most valuable aspect of your life story. You are more valuable than your job and the income you earn, or the account values you see on your computer screen. Your worth and the potential it brings are truly immeasurable throughout your lifetime, no matter what the current trend looks like. While reviewing trends, it's also very important to remember the differences between instant gratification and long-term thinking.

Investing

There is always a curve, Fed Funds Rate, interest rate, projections for the future, and noise. A lot of noise! Know the data and know that your investment accounts are going to ebb and flow much like we do. The key is knowing and understanding your plan and purpose for your account. Also know that calculated and measured changes to accounts over time are as healthy for investment accounts as they are for our personal lives. Stagnancy, procrastination, and taking a head-in-the sand approach to investing (i.e., not reviewing results) add greater risk than desired. Again, much like they do in our personal lives. This is one of the reasons why I'm determined to help people understand the significance of believing in their future, believing in their worth, and working toward a life of significance—all while leveraging money along the way.

Investing in your future is far more complex than just contributing to investment accounts. It is essential that you identify what you value most in life and support those values with best practices, even as you accept that most of life is not within your control. There is no such thing as guaranteed returns on investments, and there is no such thing as a 100 percent stress-free life. You will not find sustainable joy, happiness, resilience, peace, and awareness in your account values and growth. It's when we experience these positives in our personal life, family, valued relationships, and career that we truly learn to understand and value the long-term vision and purposes of growth in investment accounts. I share this values statement with absolute certainty: The more interest you give toward the things that matter most to you, the higher your returns will be over time.

Value of Your Time

In this chapter, we will explore the time value of money (TVM) and the importance of the value assigned to the y-axis. Money is a good gauge because it helps us see how well our actions are aligned with what we value most. As stated earlier, it's harder to earn an income, give, save, and pay taxes than it is to earn, spend money, and accrue debt. A gauge is an instrument or device for measuring the magnitude, amount, or contents of something, typically with a visual display of such information. The word *gauge* can also be used as a verb meaning to estimate or determine the magnitude, amount, or volume of something.

Money can be counted, spent, given, lost, gained, stolen, found, and earned; at every turn you can use a spreadsheet to count, estimate, and project value. We can use formulas such as time value of money (TVM) to calculate how much more valuable money is the sooner it is received.

TVM: $\mathbf{FV = PV \times [1 + (i/n)]^{(n \times t)}}$

FV = Future value of money

PV = Present value of money

i = interest rate

n = number of compounding period per year

t = number of years

A simple illustration looks like this:

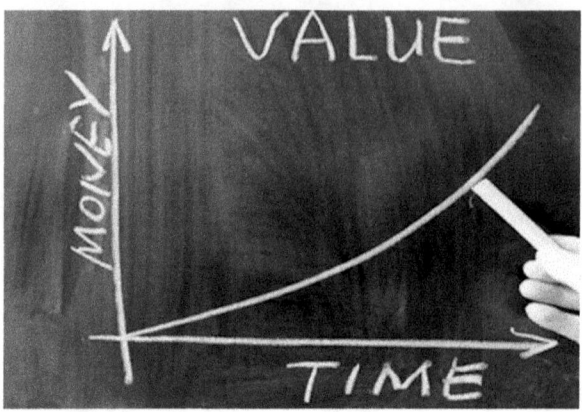

The TVM formula contains two significant variables that pertain to all aspects of our wealth: time and interest. Remember, wealth comes in various forms. Time is universal. Whether it is an hour, day, month, or year, time is the same for everyone. The only difference is whether we effectively utilize the time we are given.

But what about interest? Here are two common definitions of interest:

- From a monetary vantage point, interest is the cost of borrowing money or the profit made on investment.
- From a non-monetary vantage point, interest means to engage in or something that causes special attention to or creates arousal in someone or some personal issue.

In the TVM formula, interest is defined from a financial and economics perspective. However, in our personal lives, the two definitions of interest can be interchangeable. For example, to be interested in someone or something is different; yet when we show more interest in someone we value, growth has a higher probability of occurring, and that can be seen like interest growth in an account. To understand this better, let's swap out money from the TVM formula and replace it with relationship. Now we have a similar equation, but it's Time Value of Relationship (TVR).

When we are interested in our career, we invest time, money, education, days, nights, blood, sweat, and tears in it. And in doing so, we are betting that the value will increase over time much like the yield curve graphs. We may experience an increase in value by enjoying our career or by getting a promotion, pay raise, more responsibility, a bonus, or ownership. The enjoyment of a career, team culture, and the value delivered to clients is a qualitative value-add. It makes our career feel good and worth pursuing. The other examples are more quantitative in nature, but things like meaning, income, a bonus, and additional responsibility can be counted and measured. To know and understand the value of both is to truly be able to appreciate various aspects of life.

Remembering that wealth comes in various forms, look at the graph below and replace the y-axis (money) with one of your most valued relationships. In this example, money has been replaced with spouse. Every valuable relationship requires time to develop into a greater value. And every valuable relationship requires genuine interest and our ongoing investment to produce a higher value or return. In fact, over time, value is most often experienced via a series of increasing and decreasing values that trend upward and to the right

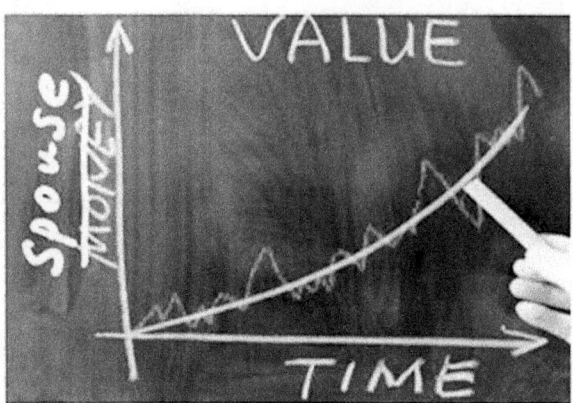

over time. Growth rarely occurs, in any aspect of life, in a consistent upward curve. This is the TVR formula at work.

If we are not taking a vested interest in (i.e., investing in) our most valued relationships, then we will most likely not see the growth we seek over time. Simply showing up is not investing. Attendance and proximity don't automatically mean being present and in the moment. Our phones prove this daily.

To fully experience and grow our TVR is to first know ourselves and how we are contributing. Just as everyone is somewhere on the leader spectrum, we are all contributing something to our most valued relationships, including our relationship with ourselves.

Application

It's extremely important to remember that seasons of growth and volatility will exist in the markets, the economy, and our career, affecting performance. It's equally important to remember that the same is true in our most valued relationships even though it's not performance quantified by a percentage. Seasons like the terrible twos in parenting and the honeymoon phase run their course. Therefore, it's wise to have predetermined strategies in place for the things and people we value most.

For example, in the investment world, it's common to think, talk, and plan for the long term with retirement accounts and legacy plans. These plans should have built-in strategies pertaining to ongoing investing percentages, portfolio construction, what-if plans, and many other practices that help us keep our eyes on the desired results. Here are several examples that helped investors during the "Housing Bubble" of 2008 and the COVID-19 pandemic. A long-term vision and its best practices promote:

- Staying invested rather than succumbing to knee-jerk reactions when volatility occurs.

- Being informed on known best practices such as "buy low, sell high." It also builds in the infrastructure to make needed investments by having cash readily available just as the best businesses do to make "smart" investments such as purchasing a competitor or making advancements in research and development.
- Filtering out noise and fearmongers that exist around every corner, selling their agendas.
- Avoiding practices that are extremely difficult, if not impossible, such as market timing. We often say we don't have a crystal ball, but emotions are powerful informants.
- Remembering what our aim is: Aim small, miss small. If someone is chasing gains that their risk-acceptance doesn't promote, then when higher than expected growth occurs, the fear of losing what was gained creeps in and adverse knee-jerk reactions may follow. Conversely, when loss happens—and it will—those who don't align risk with loss may cut bait and accept the losses rather than wait it out.

Unprecedented times such as 2008–2009 and the COVID-19 pandemic test our resolve and plans. And as Mike Tyson said, "Everyone has a plan until they get punched in the mouth." Here's the thing though, arguably one of the best heavyweight boxers to have ever competed, Mr. Tyson, competed in a sport where getting hit like he hit others, knocks opponents out cold. And if we're not careful, we can promote fear that implies the same, and the crazy thing about fear is, once we start permitting it to be our focus, the aim changes, and so do outcomes.

Instead, great planners talk about loss and gains. They prepare knowing that it's better to prepare than repair. And they adjust knowing that plans aren't etched in stone. In fact, plans should be nimble, fluid, reviewed, and discussed often. Every great team practices its plays frequently to be prepared for whatever they face. Is there a difference between sports and life? Yes and no. Both have opponents; both have wins and losses; both require practice; coaching matters, and injuries happen. The primary difference is one is a game, and the other is not. Either way, preparation is a best practice and simply showing up is not.

Wealth Coordinate: It is better to prepare than repair, and it's wise to prepare more than predict.

Finally, here's a Top 10 list of future planning topics that adults should be talking about and planning for:

1. 4Ps: Pillars of spiritual, mental, emotional, and physical health; these are four gifts to yourself and others.
2. Career: It matters to you, so talk about it and plan for it.
3. Launching children: Raising and launching successfully.
4. Us time: How are you investing in yourselves and your marriage?
5. Adult age-based changes: Our bodies, circumstances, and seasons will change. Preparing for these is a wise investment of time and proximity.
6. Empty nesting: Often a desirable thought until it hits home. Things will change and if not talked about, change may be difficult instead of rewarding.
7. Aging parents: Some want your undivided attention, and others don't want to be a burden. Either way, know your plan.
8. Retirement and its various components: Desired income, longevity, health, hobbies, activities.

9. Life of significance: You worked for decades, now what?
10. Death: Hard to talk about, which is an indication of its significance.

Be truthful in your investment evaluation of yourself. Review your tendency for productive and not so productive behaviors. Note strengths, deficiencies, and knee-jerk reactions. Look at your overall growth trend and yield curve and ask yourself what you have contributed to the upward and to the right trend you desire. Also be truthful about what aspects have hindered or deterred this desired trend. Finally, avoid the tendency to evaluate others first, whether good or bad.

If you haven't answered the values questions from the previous chapters, please pause and do so. Many of our life's best attributes and most difficult struggles can be identified by reviewing our past. Once they are identified and understood, we can then begin to invest in what is working well or divest what's not.

Regarding the management of wealth, another well-known practice is to be agnostic in investment choices by keeping the account purpose the primary focus. Said differently, it's the purpose of the account that supersedes the investment choices. Here's a brief example. To have an investment account that is predominantly one stock is known no-no. This is the antithesis of diversification. However, if the account objective is growth and the account has been growing, then someone might ask, "Why sell this one stock and buy other investments?" Valid question. However, risk lies around every corner and to invest in a variety of holdings that seek the same objective is to "diversify" risk while seeking the same objective, this scenario being growth. Visualize a snowshoe as it prevents the one wearing the shoe from sinking further into the snow. This promotes safe travel, improves efficiency, and preserves energy.

The same is true for our lives, marriages, raising children, and careers. How we invest, humble ourselves, and seek guidance for these valued relationships matters. Recognizing that others can bring value via more experience means accepting the fact that the people with whom we surround ourselves with can make us better. We can't always know what's best for us and what we value most; therefore, life is a team event. When we make "it" about ourselves above the bigger purpose, we expose ourselves to risk and potentially jeopardize what we value most. Trust and watch what happens.

Leadership

How can you use the previous TVM or TVR conversations to improve culture? Does your team know how their productivity creates the green (growth) days and counters the red (decline) days?

No one will navigate this life without struggling. Everyone will experience strife and trial. Isn't it interesting that a well-known investment practice of buy low and sell high, implies investing in down times and therefore benefiting from the growth over time. Why not apply the same principle to your personal life and pay attention to struggle rather than fear it. Why not approach aspects of life that we know are unhealthy similarly and seek help. Many households farm out the task- oriented aspects of adulthood like house cleaning, pool maintenance, and yard maintenance under the guise of saving time. Why not use professionals as the personal trainer equivalent to help improve aspects of our spiritual, mental, and emotional health as well as our financial lives?

I'm convinced that some of the mental and emotional anguish we experience is self-permitted as we have somehow accepted the lie that we can and should do most things on our own. Life is not a selfie. Think about it. What's the first thing most people do after taking a selfie—a pic of their food, a great experience, or anything else fun and exciting? They share it. Applying well-known best practices will not only help your 5Us, but it will also change your personal life.

Lifestyle Creep...

How often do you see others upgrade their lifestyle as income increases? Do you upgrade your lifestyle as your income increases? When you think of the phrase "rat race," what comes to mind?

Is it a requirement that we spend more as we make more? If what we value most is understood and discussed more frequently, is it possible that more than only one of the 5Us would see an increase from a higher income?

Lifestyle creep is like inflation, a topic we'll review soon; however inflation is the increase in cost of goods, whereas lifestyle creep is an acceptance of an increase in spending. Such an increase can become habitual because of the Law of Familiarity. This is the propensity for people to develop a fondness for things, good or bad, simply because they're familiar with them. The person who smokes when they drink but hates the smell otherwise, the one who eats sweets before bed (me, albeit frozen grapes but still), the one who spends more without awareness, the one who gives more of themselves without care for their own well-being, the one who chooses to look at the things they dislike before the things they do appreciate are examples of the Law of Familiarity at work.

Why does knowing more about lifestyle creep matter? Well, let's use a nature analogy to express the importance. Ever seen a Cheetah creep in the high grass as it approaches its soon to be prey? For a lot of us, when we see what's soon to happen, we're stirred with emotion because we know the Cheetah instinctually preys on the weak and that it's faster, more agile, and hungry. Therefore, we can predict the worst while hoping for the best.

Here's the mental hack. Before some of our most rewarding times in life, such as getting married, becoming a parent, becoming an empty nester, or entering retirement, we can familiarize ourselves with lifestyle creep and the effects of the Law of Familiarity. In doing so, we can be better prepared to support the things we value most, attend to our 4Ps, and leverage our 5Us.

When the correlation of our income to any of the 5Us goes unmonitored, there is a tendency to migrate toward an unhealthy relationship with money, metaphorically, growing blind to the importance of our income or the things we value most. This unhealthy relationship can be experienced in many ways, such as accumulating financial debt, not saving for the future, wanting to be generous but not giving, and spending that is equal to or greater than our income. When this happens, there is usually a negative correlation with our other valued relationships such as our health, family, marriage, children, and work. And as these valued relationships diminish, that tends to negatively compound other aspects of our lives, including our mental, emotional, and physical health. If not addressed, this trend introduces another version of "creep," which is gradual movement away from what we value most.

When people are in the throes of lifestyle creep, you are likely to hear statements such as, "Money is one of the top three reasons for divorce" or "Money creates unhealthy physical issues." No, it doesn't! Stop that.

Financially speaking, when there is a slide toward an undesirable direction (creep), the time value of money begins to correlate in a negative fashion. Recall our previous TVM example and replace the y-axis (money) with any other valuable relationship in your life. And now assume zero interest (i.e., whether monetary or non-monetary) and unhealthy spending patterns plus a lack of direction in this valuable relationship. What was a favorable outcome takes on a different appearance.

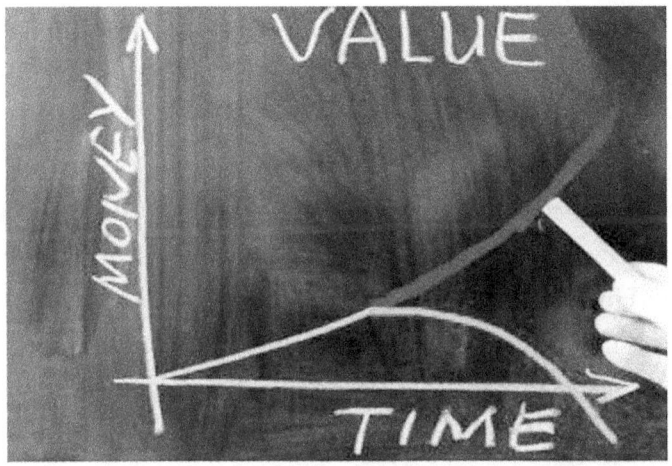

In the TVM formula, money is worth more the sooner it is received because the formula assumes the money is yielding interest (i) and compounding (n), thereby increasing its earning potential. That is, time + interest + compounding = a larger future value. Conversely, money earned or received later has less time and compounding potential and therefore experiences less return. And money that is spent or consumed without purpose (e.g., impulse purchases) often returns little to zero future value. The term *burn rate* is used to characterize such transactions because it's as if the money is simply being burned up.

At least cash reserves or money that is earmarked for "spend when ready" has a purpose and is, therefore, helpful.

The TVM principle applies to all our most valued relationships. As mentioned earlier, we can replace the y-axis (money) with spouse, children, health (4Ps), family, work, self, or other valued relationships, and the same principle will apply. Whether it's Time Value of Spouse (TVS), Time Value of Children (TVC), Time Value of Health (TVH), Time Value of Family (TVF), or Time Value of Work (TVW), they all require our ongoing investment of genuine interest (i) and the precious gift of time (n). When done well, all aspects of our valued relationships benefit from compounding growth. The question is how do we invest well? And the answer is by increasing our knowledge and learning how to apply it better by planning and investing in a brighter future.

Most of us seek a higher quality of life and when we spend time planning for and investing in areas that are valuable to us, it is amazing how the quality of our lives improves. Think with me here:

- How often have you seen improvements in areas that you value without some intentionality?
- Does your spiritual, emotional, mental, or physical health improve without intentionality?
- Do your closest relationships prosper without you intentionally investing in them?
- Does your career trend upward without you aiming toward a brighter path?

When we're not putting forth effort to plan and invest in what we value most, we promote the probability of various forms of lifestyle creep, not just the spending variety. All our most valuable relationships, such as our spiritual-physical-mental-emotional health, marriage, children, career, friendships, and yes, our 5Us, take time to develop and require an ongoing investment strategy if they are to reach their fullest potential. All of this is within your control to manage.

Applications

Leadership

Consider your team's Time Value of Relationships (TVR) and be creative with new concepts like time value of productivity (TVP). In today's remote work environments, it's critical that leaders find the proper balance between productivity and culture and understand that with distance comes the potential for mission loss. While your best producers, support staff, thinkers, and teams appreciate their individualism and privacy, for the most part, they don't want to live on islands without drawbridges. The leader's time and interest in what motivates them is critical to their success and to the direction of the organization.

Ponder this next thought and allow it to sink in: Your story is uniquely yours. No one else has your exact story, your combination of birth, upbringing, education, beliefs, values, and outcomes in life. Sure, we all share some characteristics, and I consider that a blessing. But it is important to understand that some characteristics are uniquely yours, including concepts and parts of your life that you have yet to discover or may be unwilling to uncover or restore.

As leaders, we should choose to accept that each of us is unique and that no one will ever meet all your expectations—including yourself. Quite frankly, we are all dysfunctional in some way, and accepting ourselves and others in this light will immediately decrease mental debt loads and help us all live life more abundantly.

In fact, I submit that the people with whom we have valued partnerships know that it's their combined strengths and weaknesses that make them stronger as strengths from one person overlaps the weakness of another and vice versa. Maybe this is why opposites attract. In business, having partners who possess the same strengths and weaknesses is not the best practice. Instead, having different sets of strengths increases the strength pool and, therefore, improves potential. Yes, it also increases the weaknesses pool; however, this can be offset somewhat by having a clear alignment of values, beliefs, chemistry, and purpose, which opens the door for the strengths pool to do its thing. Those in trusted partnerships and relationships are comfortable knowing and sharing their weaknesses and knowing that others possess strengths that they do not. In the best relationships, individuals don't try to make the other person like themselves but rather accept each other's differences while attempting to improve the greater good.

Wealth attributes:

- Everyone has the opportunity and potential to improve their life's trajectory.
- Experience is one of life's best teachers. Time-tested methods with large sample sizes give us reason to listen, lean into, glean from, and learn; life is not conducted in a lab or vacuum.
- Each person is uniquely created, gifted, and equipped to make a difference in their families and communities. This may sound crazy to some, but I believe the dinner table matters. TV trays are fun and convenient, but it is hard to invest in others while gazing at a device.
- Open dialogue, healthy tension, conflict resolution, and advocacy need to make a comeback. I also believe these are learned skills that require effort and time to develop.
- I believe in humankind. I also believe in God and His word.
- Life can be so much more than we make of it. As I age, I'm reminded of the brevity of life as events frame life's fragile nature.
- No one is perfect, including me, and as complex as we are, there's also some beautiful simplicity that exists all around us. I believe there is no such thing as normal. The only "normal" setting that exists in life is on the clothes washer.

From my experience in the business world and my profession, I believe that a well-known best practice in the business community holds the key to unlocking a life to be lived more abundantly. This key is like a skeleton key—one key that unlocks many different locks, such as communication, empathy, relational equity, vision creation, and more. The abundant life frequently experiences the hope statements above along with many more that were not mentioned. What I have in mind is called holistic planning, a time-tested proven concept in which successful people all over the world invest. With a few mind hacks and tweaks to traditional ongoing planning, we can use holistic planning to obtain wealth in its various forms. At the nucleus of holistic planning, there is a better quality of life. This type of planning incorporates your purpose, team, and plan; with intentionality, you can reach new heights in life even if you are already cruising at a high altitude.

So why don't more individuals, marriages, organizations, and small businesses value ongoing holistic planning? It is a well-known practice; thousands of books and articles have been written about its significance, and countless positive outcomes have been shared in writing, on screen, in testimonials, at water fountains, and watering holes. Then why isn't ongoing holistic planning part of every aspect of our lives?

Is it because of the "cheesy" signage cluttering the walls of business? Is it because it is required at work and you do not enjoy it? Is it because it is not perceived as fun? Is it because you have no experience with planning? Is it because it is difficult to conceptualize? Is it because of the lack of know-how? Is it because it does not feel rewarding? Is it because life is so fast paced that starting a plan is nearly impossible? Is it because selfishness interferes? Is it because the fear of failure creeps in before you start? Is it a combination of all these?

Yes is the answer; in fact, it is all of these and more. Ongoing holistic planning is difficult because it requires us to address what is working and what is not working. It asks us to tackle things we know we should be talking about but have not or do not want to. For married couples, the process asks them to openly communicate about difficult topics. For blended families, it asks them to openly discuss topics that concern them. For singles, it asks them to address matters that are possibly more difficult without another's help.

Also, because planning is so personal to us, it introduces a judgmental component and unfortunately, that overshadows the importance. Also, as unresolved issues in our lives are allowed to progress without being addressed or monitored, feelings of guilt, shame, or hopelessness sink to the point that a person thinks, "What's the use!?" These are common thoughts that summon up very real emotions, often visceral.

One other important aspect is planning will often revert to a quantity vibe. That is, planning is better the more money someone has. However, healthy holistic planning seeks a higher quality of life aspect and asks that the quantity support the quality.

Finally, remember that doing things yourself is limited to your knowledge, time, resources, and ability; therefore, the more trusted advisors you allow into your circle, the better. Life is not a do-it-yourself project. Ongoing holistic planning is a game changer and important enough for everyone to learn more about and discover.

Wealth Coordinate: Wealth comes in a variety of forms, as does debt, and both have beneficiaries.

- Take time to inventory your various forms of wealth discussed in later chapters of this book. This information will benefit you in ways that are difficult to explain; it will open doors and bring life to the beneficiaries, starting with you.
- Don't shy away from listing your debt instruments: Identify them and name them. This too will open doors and bring life to the beneficiaries, starting with you. Let's do our part to prevent both failure and success from dividing us, starting with ourselves.

Purpose

In previous chapters, we discussed how the income we earn flows into one of the 5Us: generosity, saving, spending, debt, and taxes. I like to illustrate this idea by looking at the human hand. Each finger symbolizes one of the uses, starting with the thumb representing generosity, the pointer finger saving, the middle finger spending, the ring finger debt, and the pinky taxes.

The 5Us exist to serve a purpose for our lives. It's the same for every home, business, nonprofit, state, and nation. Money is a resource whose purpose is to lift up, provide, purchase, pay down, be thankful, enjoy, support, leverage, build, invest, and grow planned endeavors.

And when money is used in ways that are aligned with your purpose, it works effectively to maintain and support your desired lifestyle. Similarly, a healthy hand employs all the fingers to work together for the activities we enjoy such as providing for our families, work, hobbies, serving our communities, and more.

The purpose of money is to fuel your purpose and life:
- What is your purpose?
- Have you found your purpose, and do you use it to help compass your life?
- Does your purpose support what you value most?

To help you visualize your purpose statement, here are my answers to these questions:

- Purpose: to worship, disciple, lead, and teach.
- For each of these areas, I like to create maps outlining how to get where I'd like to go. For example, to lead, teach, and disciple better, I must continue learning. So, I have a book goal for the year, and I have a content creation goal. To support these, I prefer journaling and notetaking. I'm also a fan of dictating thoughts because that helps me navigate my routines and behaviors for what I value most.
- I've created three tiers of things I value most in life to help me identify priorities and set healthy boundaries, including when I fail, mess up, or permit tier 3 things to creep into the top two tiers.

I'm also aware that some years I lived without direction. Those were times when one of the fingers was the predominant choice, and the other four took on passive roles. In those years, self was the biggest beneficiary of the spending middle finger use.

Your purpose matters. Let's find our purpose in life. Let's understand that our purpose and passions are waiting to be seen and heard. Let's address the things that will deter us from achieving our purpose and hinder our passions. Let's use the fable of the Tortoise and the Hare to learn more. If I were a betting man and did not know the outcome of this fable, I'd bet the farm on the hare, and I don't think I would be alone in that. After all, the hare is faster and more agile. Yet the hare loses the race. How is that? Well, we know how the fable goes, and this story provides a great lesson in life. I believe that figuratively speaking, we are part tortoise and part hare—the tortoise being our purpose and the hare representing our passions.

PURPOSE

Wealth Coordinate: We must be careful not to allow our passions to outpace our purpose.

Sometimes, I see a mismatch between purpose and passion, especially in the nonprofit world. Typically, nonprofit organizations do not lack passion. In fact, it's impressive how committed and driven the staff and volunteers are. But nonprofit organizations sometimes lack business acumen, vision, forecasting, and other attributes needed to run a business. Simply because it is a nonprofit organization doesn't mean it can forego best practices like running P&L statements, creating and staying on budget, and following human resources best practices. To maintain a surplus, an organization must align its purpose with a vision, steward money well, and trust its actions well enough to share how its business practices are aligned.

Conversely, most successful for-profit organizations have business acumen in spades. But mission alignment and passion sometimes waver as organizational distancing permits creep in the form of mission loss, greed, and other poor business practices. In both instances, it boils down to purpose and aim. If the nonprofit organization allows its passion to outpace its purpose, then it runs the risk of shutting its doors due to lack of funds or, worse, it foregoes its highest calling for tier 2 or tier 3 objectives. That is, contributors don't see their dollars going toward mission alignment.

Why does this matter? Because one of the primary purposes for any organization is sustainability. Businesses and organizations can't serve clients if their doors are permanently shut. The business must have sustainable business practices that ensure it will be here when it is most needed. The same is true for us. To be sustainable, we must be passionate about being present when needed, adding value, caring for the outcome of others, and taking care of ourselves.

In life you can have the attributes of both the tortoise and the hare; that is, you should have both your purpose and passions. How do we do this? Think back to the 5Us of money—generosity, saving, spending, debt, and taxes. Money is required to support all five of these aspects of our lives. The same is true of your purpose and passions. They should work in concert, like the 5Us, to provide your best life.

Let's explore how to translate what we've learned so far. In previous chapters, you've answered the first three questions listed below. Now let's apply those answers to question four:

1. What is your purpose?
2. What do you value most?
3. What are you most passionate about?
4. How are your 5Us supporting each area of your life?

Application

Mind Hack: The sequence of your thought life, which is the lens through which you view your life, surroundings, circumstances, and other key aspects, should be a trustworthy ally. Prescriptive eye wear is purchased to improve our vision, not worsen it. Your thoughts will dictate your emotions, and your emotions will stimulate your actions and behaviors. However, unless you properly define your purpose, you will run dangerously close to scenarios that figuratively or literally close your doors. But unlike the business world, you can't simply fold up shop and walk away.

Know your purpose and develop your passions that complement your bigger picture. Then understand that the sequence of your thought life is as significant to your decisions as the sequence of the 5Us are to your financial net worth. For example, if income is used without recognizing the 5Us, spending may take on a higher priority than your desired direction. Unfortunately, this often leads to a pattern that doesn't invest in our plans and our most valued relationships but simply becomes a poor spending habit. The outcome can then lead to lifestyle creep or worse.

Conversely, an organized thought life is a wealth instrument in and of itself, and it develops life routines that carry out our purpose and passions and then feeds into an organized approach with our income and our 5Us. Suggestion: Map out your 5Us and see the extent to which your use of earned income supports your purpose and the aspects of your life that you value most. Beware that sometimes, this is where self-judgment can interfere with progress. Resist that temptation; power through and seek help where needed. Remember that what you value most is worth investing in, and like investment portfolios, some investments outperform, some perform on par, and some underperform. The same is true for areas in our lives; to say that no one is perfect is to accept this as truth.

When you know that what you value most is aligned with your purpose and you know how your passions can best leverage your 5Us, life takes on a different altitude. But remember that reaching a cruising altitude requires time, energy, and navigation; it's not instantaneous. Fight the urge for instant gratification as this is also something that can creep into our lives.

Leadership

Consider these important questions: How connected to the purpose is your team? How are you discerning between purpose and passions and measuring progress? If we're not careful, we can praise ourselves for progress in important matters yet be off track relative to our purpose. Let's surround ourselves with key performance indicators that pertain to our purpose and passions and monitor both. What yield curve are you seeing, and how is your TVM, TVP (productivity), and TVR (relationship) tracking toward a yield that will be greater years from now?

Growth is gradual. It takes time to develop. We'll talk about that later.

Fiduciary

First things first. The financial services industry didn't create the concept of being a fiduciary. It adopted the concept after years of seeing greed and mismanagement of other people's assets, inappropriate illustrations, bad products, high commissions, and other poor practices. *Webster's* defines *fiduciary* as "relating to, or involving a confidence or trust such as [a] held or founded in trust or confidence, [b] holding in trust, or [c] depending on public confidence for value or currency."[3]

You would think that all parties would work in people's best interest; however, that is not true in any industry or profession. Whether we're talking about manufacturing, service providers, religion, politics, for-profit, or nonprofit, there is no profession or industry that always puts others first. There are people, however, in each of these career paths that care for others and care about the quality of their goods and services.

A word of warning to the wise: If leaders in any organization or profession consistently miss their budget, only speak of money when pressed to do so, withhold information about fees, are not transparent about costs, do not disclose commissions, or other like practices.... Houston, we have a problem. From a monetary perspective, our households should operate much like any other organization.

The difference is that organizations are producing a product or providing a service and in exchange, they are expected to make a profit or keep net assets in surplus if they are nonprofits. Although your home isn't producing or providing a tangible good or service, it is designed to create, build, and support a greater purpose. Either way, these entities operate much the same.

In its simplest form, income for the home is like top-line revenue for a business. Expenses are costs related to running the home or business. Ideally, after expenses are deducted, the home is left with discretionary income, the for-profit business is left with net income or net profit, and the nonprofit is left with surplus. Here's a visual:

Income −Necessities = Discretionary Income
- AKA budgeting for the home
- Discretionary income can then be budgeted for dining, hobbies, travel, and so on

Revenue − Expenses = Net Income, Net Profit, Net Assets or Surplus
- AKA P&L for business or nonprofit

Just because someone is responsible for leading an organization doesn't mean they manage their own assets well or that they know how to manage budgets, plan, run a P&L, or cast vision for the organization or home. And to some degree, this is acceptable but only to the extent that these shortcomings are delegated to others with the authority to manage these delegated practices properly. Knowing our strengths and weaknesses and delegating areas where we lack expertise is arguably one of the most valuable leadership traits one can possess. That's one reason that the leadership team must frequently speak to concepts related to money, monitor how well-earned revenue is aligned with purpose and mission, and steward well. When done properly, this also puts others first, in a fiduciary position.

The fiduciary role is also critical to success at home. As a fiduciary to our spouse, children, and self—arguably the three most important aspects of a home—when we put others first, it is amazing what we experience. As the old saying goes, giving starts the receiving process. Conversely, just like in the business world, when poor business practices, money decisions, or communication takes root and we stop putting others first, then . . . Houston, we still have a problem.

Application

Wealth Coordinates: In the financial services industry and in our most valued relationships, the highest standard is the fiduciary standard:

- Yes, mistakes are going to be made, and a fiduciary in either the business or the home owns the error, seeks to make things right, and seeks improvement. The other party, also being a fiduciary, accepts that no one is perfect, acknowledges the error and supports growth without judgment recognizing that they too have areas of improvement.
- Yes, things are going to happen, and the fiduciary accepts these lessons while seeking guidance from others rather than relying only on themselves. Why others? Because saying, "I got myself into this, and I'll get myself out" is narrow-minded, limited, and not seeking help from others who know more. Such an attitude becomes a debt instrument.
- Yes, let the good times roll! Please do so. Smell the roses. Listen to a baby's laugh. Smell the rain. Have a good cry. Be a good shoulder for someone else. A fiduciary understands

the importance of spiritual, mental, emotional, and physical health and recognizes that being present is one of the best ways to put others first. This is a wealth attribute.

- For help understanding the fiduciary role, think of an advisory rather than a transactional relationship. At various times, we will need both trusted advice and transactional assistance. The advisor will listen, help weed out the issues, and solve for needs, wants, and concerns. The transactional relationship will help fill voids. A quick example would be an engineer who creates blueprints that conceptualize your wishes for a new construction project. From blueprint to finished product, their role is to provide advice and to show how that advice is put into action. The general contractor, who also fills a very important role, takes the blueprints and builds what was given to them. Remember that the fiduciary is an advocate for your hopes, goals, and desires. They also assess risk, ensuring that you are informed along the way.
- Be true to and honest with yourself. This world has increasingly grown further away from many realities. For example, many people believe that everyone else is to blame for the junk that exists in their lives. Not true. Much like the false statement that money is a top reason for divorce; not accepting that we are imperfect creates its own struggles.

How are you demonstrating the character traits of a fiduciary to both the teams you lead and the organization? It's not one or the other; it's a balance of both. It can be hard, I know. One key component that is universal is communication. As we say around here, you don't have to over-communicate if you are effectively communicating.

As seasons create different time and proximity ratios for your commitments to both employer and employee, communicate often and share specifics. Have one-on-one interactions as well as group conversations. Be open to ways to improve team productivity and give others the opportunity to step up and help.

Maintaining a fiduciary role in the relationships and aspects of our lives that we value most will prove to be one of the best decisions that we can make. The process will be challenging as it requires a higher level of critical thinking and constructive thought. However, the results are without question worth the effort.

Rule of 72

When you look at your investment account statements, what are you looking for? Are you looking at the amount, whether it's up or down, or the percentage? Have you ever wondered how soon your investment account total will double?

In short, the amount of risk you apply to an investment helps determine the number of years it will take to double the account. Our risk tolerance is often referred to on a scale of conservative to aggressive, or maybe there's a number assigned to it; the higher the number the more aggressive the account.

In the investment world, to get a quick idea of how fast an account can double the Rule of 72 (R72) is used. Here's the formula:

$t = 72/r$

t = time, estimated number of years it takes to double the money

r = rate of return

Here's an example: $t = 72/6$. Answer: $t = 12$ years. In this example, it would take 12 years to double an investment if that investment consistently sees a rate of return of 6% annually. Let's first explore how this applies to gains in investment accounts. In this example, if the account was $100,000, and it saw 6% growth for 12 years, the account value would be $200,000 in roughly 12 years.

It's very important to know that the markets never provide consistent annual rates of return. Instead, rates of return vary, by the day, by the minute, and by the second. Sound familiar? The markets are as imperfect, as unpredictable and as finicky as we are.

The Rule of 72 is a quick go-to resource that helps illustrate what could be if an account earned an average rate of return. So, you may ask, what's an average rate of return? It's the good, the so-so, and the negative returns in sum, divided by the number of years. It's basically like in school when we got our test scores back, and we wondered what the average test score was. However, there is no curve to boost our rate of return.

For example:
5% + 0% + –2% + 7% + 7% + 4% + –1% = 2.86%

Also know that this calculation reflects your rate of return, i.e., your account, and not the comprehensive stock or bond market return. Returns on other investments may be shown for comparison and are referred to as benchmarks.

Finally, we should determine what amount of risk is best for the specific purposes of the investments we own rather than what someone else would choose for their risk profile—not your neighbor, not your parents, not your direct report, not even the person managing your money. It is your account, not theirs. Help is helpful; guidance is appreciated. However, when it comes to the income you earn and the investments you make, it is the combination of the risk you are willing to take, per the timeline you chose, and the purpose of the investment that matters.

When an account is earmarked for a specific purpose, it should be managed specifically for that purpose rather than a general purpose.

RULE OF 72

It is not uncommon to have various accounts geared for specific purposes, with different rates of return.

The Rule of 72 also applies on the flip side, aka interest owed. For instance, the Rule of 72 is also applicable to interest on a mortgage, vehicle loan, credit cards, or any other debt that charges interest. However, there is a distinct difference between gains and interest owed on debt.

Some debt is referred to as "good" debt, implying it's helpful somehow. For example, mortgage interest might be considered "good" because a home is valuable. Another example could be a business loan; it may be considered "good" because the loan provides working capital for expansion or growth. Either way, it's important to remember that interest owed is hard-earned income (home) or revenue (business) going to someone else (the lender). Debt is still debt, good or bad, justified or not—whether the interest is high or low; it's best to get it off the books. Furthermore, it's best to avoid it all together if it is used as an extension of income, as credit cards are.

A basic definition of interest says that interest is the cost of money. Here's an example of the Rule of 72 related to simple interest owed on debt:

$t = 72/15$

$r = 15\%$ (a lower-than-average interest owed on credit cards)

$t = 4.8$ years

Stop, collaborate, and listen. This is not vanilla, but this is as cold as ice to your potential. When purchases are made on high interest credit cards, the amount purchased compounds with the interest. In this example, assuming no payments, the original amount is four times greater in less than five years! Now you can see why high interest loans are highly profitable to the lender. But you are the beneficiary of the interest owed on the debt; this is also a great reminder of why it's beneficial to have higher credit scores. Don't hate the player; hate the game. I want you to despise the fact that debt, monetarily and in its various forms, is something that can lure, divide, and ultimately create tension in valued relationships.

Furthermore, there is no beneficial retail marketing tactic that is geared toward you, the customer. It doesn't matter if we're talking about points for airlines, 0 percent balances, or famous celebrities speaking about the value, retail lenders are marketing a product known as a loan, and it is a numbers game with high stakes. Recently, I heard someone say that their goal was to never pay interest on a credit card in their life. That's someone who plans to leverage the system rather than being leveraged. Aim small; miss small.

Another example I often refer to is the amortization schedule on your mortgage. In fact, to help you remember, let's use word association and remember to "AMOR" (i.e., love) your amortization schedule. I want you to figuratively "love" the fact that you know exactly what you will pay on a mortgage. Here's why. For a 30-year mortgage at an interest of 5.3%, no matter the purchase amount, the owner will pay as much in interest as they did for the home.

For example, on a $350 thousand house purchased, at 5.3% over 30 years, the total amount paid will be a few hundred dollars shy of $700 thousand. Do the math, it's the same across the board, no matter the amount borrowed. The only exceptions would be based on the amount of the downpayment or whether extra payments are made, but still, the amount of interest will be substantial.

Is this "good"? Investing in our families, marriages, and ourselves is always good. Knowing what the costs are for the investment and ascertaining the best way to invest in what matters most to us is better. It's also important to remember that "providing" doesn't imply a bigger home or more stuff. And most likely, it will never imply taking on massive amounts of debt.

Application

There is no magic investment that consistently provides high results year after year—whether you're considering stocks, bonds, speculative investments, precious metal, real estate, or cash equivalents. It doesn't exist. The same is true of ourselves and our personal relationships.

We should expect volatility in our portfolios. It is going to happen unless you invest in cash, which, most of the time, means being on the sidelines and comes with its own deficits. However, you should also expect growth, and if you remove the ups and downs, as shown in our TVM graph, you should see a curve that trends up and to the right and has an accounting color of green over several years.

Shouldn't the same apply to our personal growth and our most valued relationships? Think back to the "normal" yield curve. Don't we all want a curve that looks similar for all things in life? The level at which we invest in our most valued relationships will help determine the return that we should expect, much like what we expect for conservative to aggressive investment portfolios. Equally important, the degree to which we invest in ourselves will dictate the return we should expect over time.

As an adult, our life, marriage, parenting, career, income, friendships, and 4Ps are all beneficiaries of the effort we put toward them. And I'm not simply referring to continuing education credits that you breeze through because you must. Intentionality creates far greater outcomes than checking boxes. When was the last time you thought about how the quality of your marriage or your relationship with your children will double over time? We can "double double" the quality of our most valued relationships, or we can decrease the net worth of our most valued relationships by adding debt instruments.

Also remember that with the Rule of 72, each new addition or contribution to an investment account will experience a new R72 because its time is newer, and most likely its price per share is different. The same is true in our relationships as trust, loyalty, and love develop over time. Other than the example of love at first sight, most of the time, it takes years to develop characteristics that deepen relationships, and during those years, we often experience some volatility—just like we do in our investment accounts. Invest in the relationally volatile times rather than selling and be rewarded with the outcomes!

This is important for several reasons. First, it's common to make on-going contributions to our investment accounts. For example, we may contribute to our 401(k) every pay period. Second, it's natural to feel that growth curves should be smooth in our investment accounts, and it's also natural to feel the same for our lives. But it isn't, and it won't be.

It's also natural to feel that the simple interest "like" returns we see from a CD or Treasury Bill act the same as investing in our closest relationships. It is possible to see short-term gains in our accounts, ourselves, and others; however, if the purpose of the investment is growth, the timeline is long-term, and we should guard against the tendency to seek instant gratification. Instant gratification is more transactional, and from an investment perspective, this is more like an income purpose rather than growth. We'll talk more about interest shortly.

Using an R = 7%, compounding looks like the following:

- Jan. 2024 contribution of $10 = $20 in 2034 with 7% growth
    - » Additional contribution of $10 in Jan. 2025
      = $20 in 2035 with 7%
    - » Additional contribution of $10 in Jan. 2026
      = $20 in 2036 with 7%

» Additional contribution of $10 in Jan. 2027
= $20 in 2037 with 7%
  » Additional contribution of $10 in Jan. 2028
  = $20 in 2038 with 7%
    » Additional contribution of $10 in Jan. 2029
    = $20 in 2039 with 7%
      » Additional contribution of $10 in Jan. 2030
      = $20 in 2040 with 7%
        » Sum total of $140 with $70 invested

Staying patient with all aspects of growth is a key strategy. We'll talk more about this in the chapter devoted to various aspects of growth. For now, remember that you should expect growth over time. Also know that growth mongers exist in many places, and they take on a similar appearance to the social media posts that illustrate a life that appears to always be perfect. Know this: Life is not perfect. It's also important to note that pictures taken after all the work is done, don't reflect all the risk taken. Just the reward.

Keep in mind that when you pour into others who may never be able to repay you, the investment you're pouring into them is a gift. You don't like gifts with strings attached, and they don't either. As it pertains to our children, it's best to remember that no one is born mature. Instead, we grew into and out of our terrible twos, preschool, teenage, and college years over time. We were taught about electricity, eating, walking, reading, doing math, and communicating with others; all that took time. None of us grew up overnight contrary to what Grandma said as she pinched your cheeks.

Understanding how the Rule of 72 can help predict long-term investment growth and help define investment account purposes. This tool is also very helpful for dealing with the wealth and debt aspects of life.

Wealth Coordinates:

- Interest owed is the equivalent of our hard-earned income going toward someone else's earned income. Use the Rule of 72 to see how much of your income is going toward someone else's lifestyle. Quick side note: This also helps us see the full cost of instant gratification decisions. For example, if something costs $1,000 and in total $1,350 was paid with interest, was it worth the full cost?
- As we create parallels to our personal lives, the Rule of 72 also helps us:
  » Conceptualize how our investments in what we value most can look over time—how we can double the double. Keep reading.
  » Conversely, the Rule of 72 also helps us see why self-induced debt does not promote growth for anyone, including ourselves.

Leadership

How can you apply the Rule of 72 principle to your team and business? Think about the differences in team members and how each has a different rate of return. This isn't a bad thing; it's useful. It's wise to make sure that skill sets line up with responsibilities. To have someone in a role that doesn't align with their giftedness or strengths is no different than an investor expecting aggressive growth when the investment manager is using a conservative portfolio. Neither is healthy.

It's important to be content with the fact that not everyone wants the same career trajectory. This deserves ongoing conversations with our teams. Many people in the workforce are perfectly satisfied with their role, income, and effort. Don't minimize; instead, maximize this working partnership. That's your role as the leader.

Inflation

Do you remember when gas was less expensive and vehicles were reasonably priced? In a nutshell, the upward shift in prices over time demonstrates the effects of inflation. In the US, the dollar bill still represents 100 pennies, but those 100 pennies have lost their buying power over time. For example, something that cost $10 five years ago now cost $12.20; so instead of 1,000 pennies, it now requires 1,220 pennies.

The closest analogy to inflation in relation to our human body is the effects of aging, and as we know, those effects usually increase during different seasons of our lives. For example, we don't think about metabolism in our twenties, and we shudder at our parents and their friends talking about their health issues while at dinner when we are in our thirties. Then, it's funny how one day, you and your friends start talking about the number of times you wake up at night to go the restroom or about your blood pressure, or whatever!

Just like the conversation that starts with, "Hey, you remember when this only cost ten bucks?!" It's no secret that as we grow older, our aging has side effects, which come in various forms as our abilities slowly decline. We experience slow decline in our eyesight, hearing, physical abilities, and physical characteristics. We also see our emotional and mental capacities change as stress or "life" happens. Also, in some scenarios, we see mental and emotional margin decline in loved ones as illness or age takes what was theirs. Something very important to note here is that much of this decline is due to our actions and surroundings more than it is about our physical abilities gradually declining. Stress is a very costly debt instrument that has highly inflated effects on our health and most valued relationships.

Monetarily, inflation is best defined as the gradual and sometimes sharp increase in the cost of goods and services. As we discussed in our example, it's the difference in the cost of goods and services year over year (YOY). Here's a graph from the US Bureau of Labor Statistics that illustrates the past several decades of inflation in the US:

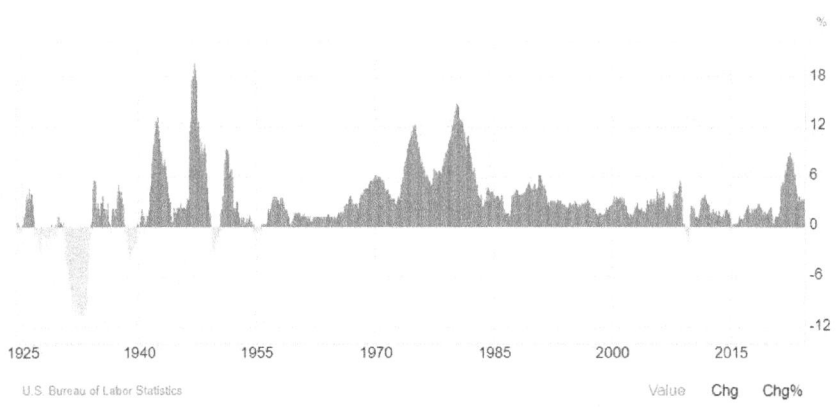

Since 2020, we've seen a sharp spike in costs across the board, and the inflationary season has been stickier than expected. Note the spikes over the past fifty or so years dating back to 1970. I remember the late '70s and early '80s. I also remember talking with my parents about the double-digit "A" paper mortgage they had for the home I grew up in. Crazy! Think about that. If a 5.3% mortgage doubles the cost paid for a home in 30 years, what about a15% mortgage! I also remember what I paid for my first truck and home; neither of them is within earshot of today's prices. And, for the record, I didn't walk uphill both ways to school; I rode the bus until I could drive.

Inflation is real and a common process in all aspects of our lives. One quick observation: Notice what you don't see much of in the graph, deflation. That's represented by the yellowish color. In my day-to-day world, we often refer to inflation as the silent killer of comprehensive planning. Here's why. For the most part, those who are forty or older have experienced cost of living increases. Like my examples of my first truck and home, they've seen how everything from what they buy at the grocery store to their insurance has increased, and they have a benchmark for comparison. This is good; experience is helpful.

If we've experienced this, then why is inflation a silent killer of planning? Because there are many differences between the accumulation phase and the distribution phase of life; that is between the working years and retirement. There's also a difference between experiencing something and being able to recall it versus planning for an unknown variable. Look at the graph again. Besides the rare event of deflation, what else do you see? Do you see any consistency? Not really.

Do you see a predictable trend? Yes. We can predict that inflation is more probable than deflation, and it is going to fluctuate while it continues to increase year over year (YOY). Why does all this matter? Let's use this watered-down inflation illustration to help visualize the concept:

- Inflation is the increase of cost Year Over Year (YOY).
- If something costs $100 this year and for whatever reason experiences a 5% increase to produce or provide, it will cost $105.
- During the following year, if that same product experiences a 2% increase in inflation, what was $105 will cost $107.10.

- And the pattern continues at a pace that is variable. Meaning inflation does not have a predictable annual amount by percentage; yet it is more likely to occur than not.

Let's use the graph again and review the three largest spikes since 1970. Those spikes range from 9.1% in 2022 to 14.8% in 1980. You might be saying OK, I see it; I don't like it, but I see it. But why? Why does it seem like everything keeps getting more expensive? The macro answer is far more complex and for others much smarter than me. My purpose in sharing this hasn't changed. Our money speaks to us in various ways, and we can use what it teaches us to learn more about life, our 5Us, and the things we value most.

Application

Here's what inflation teaches us. Remembering lifestyle creep, the Law of Familiarity, and Rule of 72, let's look at what we have learned and see how we can hack the system for our benefit.

Let's start with the Rule of 72. I like this quick resource because it works in so many ways. Remember, inflation is not a consistent flat amount annually, and neither are our investments and self-growth. However, we can use this rule to help illustrate important aspects. Let's look at what inflation looks like over time:

- 72 / 2 = 36
  - » Something that inflates in cost annually at 2% will double in cost in 36 years.
  - » Meaning, if it costs $1 now, it will cost $2 in 36 years.
- 72 / 6 = 12
  - » Something that inflates in cost annually at 6% will double in cost in 12 years.
  - » Meaning, if it costs $1 now, it will cost $2 in 12 years, $4 in 24 years, and $8 in 36 years.

- 72 / 12 = 6
    - » Something that inflates in cost annually at 12% will double in cost in 6 years.
    - » Meaning, if it costs $1 now, it will cost $2 in 6 years, $4 in 12 years, $8 in 18 years, $16 in 24 years, $32 in 30 years, and $64 in 36 years.

Now let's talk about lifestyle creep and the Law of Familiarity and how they relate to inflation.

Wealth Coordinates:

- It's safe to say that something that slowly doubles in cost over thirty-six years will most likely get lost in the shuffle. Sometimes, it may feel like a rounding error, and we don't even recognize it; think subscriptions or lower cost monthly items that are on autopay. However, something that doubles in cost in twelve years will more likely be noticed, and something that doubles every six years should definitely be on the radar.
- Lifestyle creep has a way of sneaking into our lives like the thirty-six-year example. It's like waking up one day and saying, "What happened?" or "When did we start going in different directions?" The six- or twelve-year example might spark a mild assessment such as, "We don't make enough money." Lifestyle creep is not as sneaky as inflation when we're investing in what we value most. It's also more noticeable when we experience sharp increases as in the 12-percent inflation example.
- The Law of Familiarity is also sneaky, and it's elusive. It can take on a different appearance over time and give the illusion that something we like or love doesn't appeal to us anymore

as the effects of the aging dollar, aging stuff, aging self, or lengthier relationships carry on. We can temper the effects of the Law of Familiarity with awareness and by investing in what we value most.

The following topics explore several areas in which we can increase our awareness of the effects of inflation.

Lifestyle

Inflation is going to happen. It's helpful to remember that what we're trending toward with our 5-U patterns is amplified by this silent killer and by the fact that most of what we purchase is either consumed or depreciates in value. Think about that for a few minutes without judging yourself or anyone else. Most of the things we use our income for decrease in value over time, or they are consumed like food or drink. There are four common exceptions: home, investments, relationships, valued experiences, and giving.

We know that many people don't like the term *budgeting*, and I get it, but if we're not budgeting, then what is going to help the home operate better over the long term? Develop your plan with long-term objectives and allow it to be pliable. Rigidity is good for structures; yet there is something to be said about the engineering of structures in highly volatile areas.

Leadership

Knowing whether your team(s) is gaining or losing ground to productivity is part of the leader's role. After all, the best leaders are like the bulldozer that goes before the team, removing as many obstacles to growth as possible. Truth is, inflation hits all of us in different ways, in different amounts, and at different times. Be a fiduciary to the person who is hurting. Learn what empathy is and apply it more frequently. The role of a leader goes far beyond numbers.

Four Pillars of Health

The four pillars of our health—spiritual, mental, emotional, and physical—are crucial. We talked about the effects of aging on our physical and mental health earlier in this chapter. Of these four pillars, one of them will diminish more as we age; whereas the others have the potential to increase in value. The physical pillar slowly diminishes before the others, and it is the pillar most often used to compare ourselves with other people, or it's the most sought-after or displayed pillar.

We are all capable of being mental athletes, or what I sometimes refer to as "small business owners of ourselves." Our physical nature is going to decline over time. Period, end of story. Accepting this inflationary thought is truth in love. However, the other three pillars have a much longer shelf life, and they help us combat inflation like investment accounts do with growth. How are you investing in your four pillars?

Valued Relationships

In our most valued relationships, creep and familiarity are going to occur, especially in relationships that are closest to us. One of the keys, much like purpose for the investment account, is to know "what" you value most and to invest and protect that with your actions and routines. For example:

- Being an empty nester is something to look forward to, but this season can vary by parent. While one parent may like the thought of a decrease in expenses, the other parent may miss the proximity of children; therefore, this can be a vulnerable time in a marriage. Yet with awareness, couples can talk about what lies ahead and prepare. They can talk about fears, concerns, and what excites them most about this season of life. After all, this should be an exciting time as the home successfully launches a young adult.

- Retirement is a thought that most people value but as the joke goes, "We married each other for breakfast and dinner but not for lunch." Retirement raises the question, "What do we do with all this 'free' time together?" The COVID-19 pandemic showed us that spending all day with those we love most has its challenges. The early stages of retirement are a vulnerable time. It's healthy to find shared interests and hobbies and also maintain activities that can be done independently. An unhealthy balance of one or the other has the potential to create some emotional and mental debt.

Knowing how our "cost" of living takes on more than a monetary aspect is crucial. Nothing will stay the same for your entire life. Procrastination, idleness, and staying on the shores of life have risks and costs, so do living out over our skis, leaving wakes, and running on full tilt. Find the balance, trust the process, and remember that life is not a DIY project.

Everything in our life will change over time, so knowing what you love and what you value most is one of life's greatest treasures. Also knowing that the people you love will change over time, as you do, is equally important. As C. S. Lewis wrote, "It is much better fun to learn to swim than to go on endlessly (and hopelessly) trying to get back the feeling you had when you first went paddling as a small boy."[4] The sooner we accept that change is beneficial, the sooner we'll open our eyes, minds, and hearts to a brighter tomorrow.

To embrace change is to know and understand that you and everything around you will gradually be different. Such awareness is healthy, helpful, and wealthy. We like ripe fruit. We enjoy flowers in full bloom. We like wine, bourbon, and scotch that age over time. Paintings are more valuable the older they are and after the artist is deceased. All these take time to develop. It's generally the stuff that depreciates that we like new and shiny. Let's not confuse the two.

Interest

Compounding Interest

Sometimes referred to as the Eighth Wonder of the World, compounding interest is the growth of growth without any additions or contributions to the principal over a specified period. To help visualize the concept of compounding, let's check out an old favorite and that's the penny that doubles every day for a month. If you haven't heard this before, guess the answer to this question:

How much is one cent worth if it doubles daily for 30 days? What's your guess?

The answer is: five million, three hundred sixty-eight thousand, seven hundred nine dollars and twelve cents.

What! Yes, that's right: $5,368,709.12!

And that's exactly the reason why compounding interest is a popular concept in the financial services industry. Here's the chart to review:

$	0.01
$	0.02
$	0.04
$	0.08
$	0.16
$	0.32
$	0.64
$	1.28
$	2.56
Day 10 $	5.12

$	10.24
$	20.48
$	40.96
$	81.92
$	163.84
$	327.68
$	655.36
$	1,310.72
$	2,621.44
Day 20 $	5,242.88

$	10,485.76
$	20,971.52
$	41,943.04
$	83,886.08
$	167,772.16
$	335,544.32
$	671,088.64
$	1,342,177.28
$	2,684,354.56
Day 30	$5,368,709.12

This gives a whole new meaning to find a penny, pick it up . . .

OK, so you're not going to double something every day, but I'm sharing this to prove a concept. Compounding exists, and the timeline may vary depending upon the investment purpose and investment type. Compounding is also available in our most prized assets known as strengths, gifts, talents, and valued relationships.

For the growth of assets, we've already talked about compounding with the Rule of 72. Let's do a quick review. As interest, yield, dividends, and growth are experienced in our investment portfolios, we can experience growth of the growth from previous years. Think of momentum being built upon momentum. Stay tuned, the double-double explanation is coming.

Remember from our conversation about TVM, the sooner we begin investing, the better. Why? Because of growth and then compounding the growth. Also remember, the sooner we take an interest in things that better our lives, the sooner interest can be made and start compounding.

Tales you win with compounding growth. Heads you lose with compounding debt interest. Have you ever wondered why it's extremely difficult to get out from under high interest loans? As we learned with the Rule of 72, compounding debt interest works the same way as compounding growth except in reverse from your point of view. With debt it's not your money that's growing; it's the amount you owe that's compounding like the penny example.

Take for example a $5,000 credit card debt with 28% interest, which is a typical interest rate in higher-than-average interest rate environments.

Scenario #1 of a $5K debt with 28% interest:
- Paying $125 per month would take 9.8 years to pay off the principal amount.
- The total amount paid is $9,676.12 (almost twice the original amount) in return for borrowing $5K.

Scenario #2 of a $5K debt with 28% interest:
- Paying $117 per month would take 21.3 years to pay off the principal amount.
- The total amount paid is $24,729.81 (five times the original amount) in return for borrowing $5K.

OUCH! That's crazy. You know what's also crazy? Debt instruments like self-doubt, perfectionism, comparison, and other debt robbing instruments compound at similar rates. I understand seasons of difficulty exist; trust me.

I've fought depression. I've felt shame. I know what an anxiety attack feels like. I also know it is helpful to address things that hinder progress while seeking professional help and being honest with ourselves and others. We must talk about this. We must address the mental and emotional health issues we have in the world today because these well-known debt instruments compound daily like the example of the penny, operating the same as debt, just not in fiscal form. Much like poor conversation leads to strained partnerships, not talking and addressing debt instruments like these often leads to poor spending, eating, and other unhealthy behaviors.

Once I recognized where some of my faults originated, I was comforted by the fact that I was further along my growth journey than I thought. Here's what I mean. Counseling helped me see that during my childhood, I was exposed to great, good, and poor patterns. The great and good patterns were helpful, but the poor ones were hurtful. To me, this was a watershed moment because I learned that I didn't create some of my poor behaviors; rather I inherited them; I was the beneficiary of poor patterns. And yes, the opposite was helpful too. I inherited many wealthy attributes and now I can build upon them. Remember, wealth and debt come in various forms and both have beneficiaries.

From trusted professionals and close relationships, I learned that I could get rid of these debt instruments easier because I didn't create them. Much like gifts we've received for birthdays and Christmas that we don't like or need, we can also choose what to do with these teachings, and you don't need a gift receipt or permission to discard them.

I also learned that regifting debt instruments, giving them back, or passing them down is detrimental. And instead, I can choose to give myself a better gift by recognizing the problem, accepting the teaching, and then correcting them mentally, emotionally, physically, and spiritually. In turn, this utilizes various forms of wealth-like awareness, forgiveness, love, acceptance, and other wealth instruments that then begin compounding growth. Being

INTEREST

a fiduciary with my best interests pays dividends not only for me but also for others around me, and the math is amazingly beneficial. Here's an illustration using money to demonstrate the parallel:

- Earlier we looked at a debt of $5K with 28% and monthly payments of $125. Outcome = 9.8 years to pay off and a total amount paid of $9,676.12.
- Now let's review the opposite situation: A $5K investment account, that has a monthly contribution of $125 for 9.8 years, growing at an average rate of return of 7%. The account value would be $29,861.67. (See chart below from Investor.gov.)

Poor illustrations of unachievable growth have been used in this industry for decades. I will not contribute to the cause by using unreasonable growth percentages.

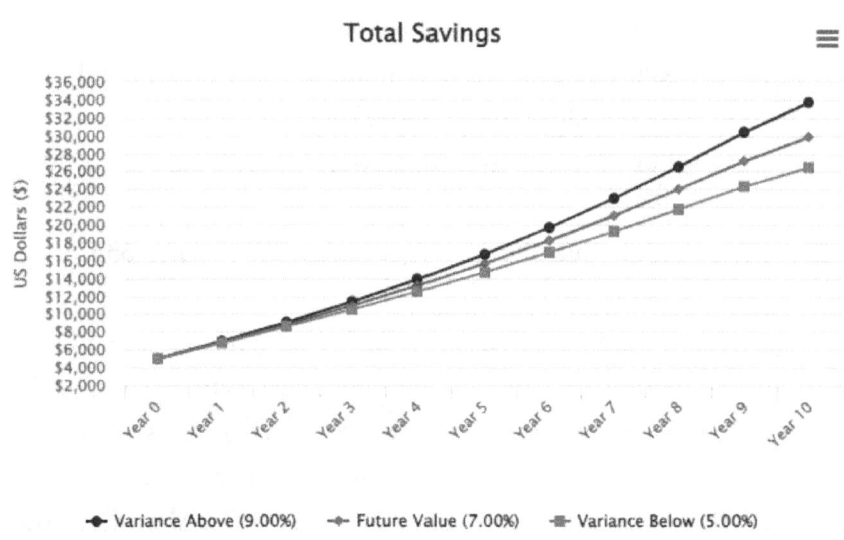

THE TWO SIDES OF EVERY DOLLAR

Note that the graph shows 5%, 7%, and 9% growth over 10 years. Here are the various outputs:
- At year 9, the 9% amount is $30,391, the 7% amount is $27,159, and the 5% amount is $24,296.
- At year 10, the 9% amount is $33,749, the 7% amount is $29,861, and the 5% amount is $26,457.

Here's what this helps illustrate. Note the spread variance in the investing compared to the debt owed.
- **Debt:** $4,676 of hard-earned income was paid toward interest over a 10-year span. Total payment of original $5K plus interest is $9,676.
- **Growth:** Conversely, over a 10-year span, keeping the same monthly payment of $125, a total of $15,000 would be added to the $5K, and the differences shown are the growth.
- That's a spread of roughly $34K on the low end and $43K on the high end. By spread, I'm referring to the difference between total debt paid to someone else ($9,676) and total investment plus growth in one's own account.
    - Low end: the spread between -$9,676 and $24,296 = ~$34K.
    - High end: the spread between -$9,676 and $33,749 = ~$43K.
- This visual also illustrates the loss in personal potential as we permit debt instruments to linger versus investing in ourselves physically, mentally, emotionally, and spiritually.
- Finally, in a way, this is a visual of the parable of talents (Matthew 25:14–30) except that no line is shown for the one person who didn't invest the talents he was given. When

his master returned, he would have the original $5K minus inflation; whereas the others countered inflation, doubling the investment. With the Rule of 72 variable of 7%, we know that without any additions, the money almost doubles in 10 years.

In the parable of talents, each was given according to their ability. So, who would you invest in?

Remember that the sequence of your thought life matters just as much as account growth. Compounding interest can be one of our best allies and strengths. Kick the thoughts that deflate to the curb, recognizing that we all have areas that could use some growth. It's also wise to remember that when our strengths aren't attended to, there are potential built-in struggles. For example, as confidence gives way to arrogance, what was a wealth instrument and growing in value can start accruing debt.

Simple Interest

This form of interest is also helpful. Let's look at the primary difference between compounding and simple interest. Simple Interest is calculated on the amount deposited or owed over a specified period:

> I = PxRxT
> Interest = Principal (invested or borrowed) x Rate x Time (specified period)

In our penny example, compounding interest is what made the owner of the penny a multi- millionaire. It wasn't the original principal amount. Here's a simple interest example:

> Principal of $100 x Rate 5% x Time 3 Years = $15

I know, compounding interest is much more attractive. However, that also helps illustrate the point. How well are we investing in our accounts, others, and ourselves?

This simple interest calculation is sometimes used to help project a high-level income illustration for retirement purposes. For example, there is a concept known as the 4% Rule that suggests a retiree can safely withdraw 4% from their retirement portfolio annually, adjusting for inflation, and not run out of money.

Here's something very important to note: This concept assumes that the account that is being withdrawn from is invested and not just sitting in cash. There are two reasons why this note is very important and should never be overlooked. Let's review using the following example. Let's say that cash is getting only .02% in the bank and inflation for a given year is at 2%. Remember, cash sitting idle almost always loses to inflation:

- From a retirement *income* perspective, if a retirement account is sitting idle in cash and getting, I can't say earning, getting only 0.02% and inflation is 2% for a given year, this illustrates a loss in purchasing power at a rate of 1.98% (.02% increase –2% Inflation = –1.98%). Therefore, in this example, as income is withdrawn from this cash account for cost of living, in theory, a higher percentage withdrawal will be required annually to keep up with inflation as purchasing power declines.
- From a *growth* perspective, using the same variables, if a retirement account only sees .02% average annual growth and inflation is at 2%, then in theory the account value has depreciated by 1.98% more than the actual account value shown.

Let's use a different growth percentage to stress the importance of attempting to mitigate inflation with a higher annual average percentage rate of return. Using a hypothetical 5% growth rate and inflation at 2%, then in theory the account growth was more along the lines of 3% (5% growth minus 2% inflation = 3%).

Application

What part of your life are you OK with losing 1.98% of its value annually? Are you OK with your accounts decreasing at this rate annually? What about the distance in your relationships, in your marriage, or with your children or friends? What about your health or your career?

With only a few exceptions, the value of all the items we purchase depreciates annually, especially if we take out a loan or borrow to purchase them. This is why it is important to understand the difference between appreciation and depreciation. Both exist, and they have an exchange rate that varies by season and by person. However, by understanding the difference and where the differences exist, we have a better chance at combatting depreciation and leveraging appreciation.

So back to the question: In what part of your life are you OK with having the quality or quantity decrease annually? We can accept that our bodies gradually age, but we can also invest in them, which helps combat the decline and, in theory, prolongs life. In so doing, we function as a fiduciary for ourselves and those we love. In most countries, we get to choose what adds and what depreciates value; therefore, we can exercise some control, while remembering that change is constant. For less than desirable circumstances, we can accept our failures and the associated costs. For those who seek spiritual growth, you can take ground by believing God's promises and investing your life accordingly.

We have the option to be the best mental athletes possible and, therefore, be the best version of ourselves as we invest in the various aspects of our lives. Remembering that our home, investments and relationships all have the potential to trend upward and to the right as we accept that change is a constant, that no one is perfect, and that no one "wins" all the time.

Wealth Coordinate: Understanding the correlation or ratio of change to growth is helpful. I'm not advocating change for the sake of change, but change that is useful, measurable, and on purpose. Each of us has one or more aspect of our life that would benefit from change. It's also useful to know what areas of our life are currently in growth mode.

Leadership

Our team(s) has a qualitative interest-like component. By this I mean, it's hard to measure some aspects of our teams; however, there is always growth or decline somewhere, and leaders must address those matters. If it's a wealth-related circumstance where more support could fuel compounding growth, find it. Invest in it, clear the obstacles, and get out of the way. If it's a debt-related issue, weed it out while also looking in the mirror. Sometimes, the cost of debt-related interest is us.

Change that is purposeful promotes health and wealth in its many forms. And, yes, the other side of the coin is also true. By not accepting or promoting change that is useful and purposeful, we promote a negative ratio and, therefore, accept the promotion of depreciation in the aspects of life that we value most. It may be difficult to accept that debt often pays the lender better and faster than growth flows to the account owner. Take an amortization schedule for example. This is why I ask all homeowners to "amor" their schedule. Here's a visual for the example used earlier with a $350K loan at 5.3% for 30 years.

INTEREST

Year	Interest	Principal	Ending Balance
1	$18,432.34	$4,890.46	$345,109.54
2	$18,166.75	$5,156.04	$339,953.50
3	$17,886.75	$5,436.05	$334,517.45
4	$17,591.53	$5,731.26	$328,786.19
5	$17,280.29	$6,042.51	$322,743.68
6	$16,952.14	$6,370.66	$316,373.02
7	$16,606.17	$6,716.63	$309,656.39
8	$16,241.41	$7,081.38	$302,575.01
9	$15,856.85	$7,465.95	$295,109.06
10	$15,451.40	$7,871.40	$287,237.66
11	$15,023.93	$8,298.87	$278,938.80
12	$14,573.24	$8,749.55	$270,189.25
13	$14,098.09	$9,224.71	$260,964.54
14	$13,597.12	$9,725.67	$251,238.86
15	$13,068.96	$10,253.84	$240,985.02
16	$12,512.10	$10,810.69	$230,174.33
17	$11,925.01	$11,397.78	$218,776.55
18	$11,306.04	$12,016.76	$206,759.79
19	$10,653.45	$12,669.35	$194,090.44
20	$9,965.42	$13,357.38	$180,733.07
21	$9,240.02	$14,082.77	$166,650.30
22	$8,475.24	$14,847.56	$151,802.74
23	$7,668.92	$15,653.88	$136,148.86
24	$6,818.81	$16,503.99	$119,644.87
25	$5,922.53	$17,400.26	$102,244.61
26	$4,977.58	$18,345.21	$83,899.40
27	$3,981.32	$19,341.48	$64,557.92
28	$2,930.95	$20,391.85	$44,166.07
29	$1,823.54	$21,499.26	$22,666.81
30	$655.98	$22,666.81	$0.00

Note that the interest paid in the first 10 years is roughly $170K, and the amount paid toward the principal is roughly $62K. That's almost a 1:3 ratio of investment to paying someone else. Let's now flip the script and look at the opposite hypothetical. Let's say someone invested $62K and saw $170K in 10 years; that's an R72 value that almost triples in 10 years. This is also roughly a 1:3 ratio;

however, it's one part contribution, and the rest is all growth. That would be great to see in an investment account. Which would you prefer, paying someone else $170K or tripling your own original investment?

Here's the hope with this visual. We all know that relationships are sometimes difficult; so is home ownership. All our valued aspects of life come at a cost. The schedule that I want you to love shows the cost of home ownership; whereas the costs related to our valued relationships of self, spouse, children, family, friends, coworkers, and neighbors don't. However, knowing how costly they are and whether they're functioning like interest paid to someone else (first example) or like growth (second example) can make all the difference in the world.

Great investments take time to develop while debt, like this amortization schedule shows, is more of a struggle than helpful. If we're quick to say we all have baggage that we carry, then how are we addressing it with others and ourselves and making it more of an investment conversation.

When we're apt to listen, money has a way of teaching us a lot about ourselves and our surroundings.

Your Strategy Matters (to Your Money and Your Life)

A few common strategies are used to invest, grow, and accumulate assets in investment accounts. There is some overlap but, for the most part, each of the three major strategies is distinct. Interestingly, these financial management strategies have characteristics that apply to life beyond financial matters. Before we review these strategies, it's important to know that for this illustration, we're not referring to income or dividend strategies. We're also not referring to the differences between stocks, bonds, mutual funds, or ETFs. These are all helpful, and each has their place. In this chapter we will review three of the more common methods to contribute, manage, and grow accounts.

Dollar Cost Averaging

Dollar Cost Averaging (DCA) is a well-known and widely practiced purchasing method in the investment industry. For example, when an employee contributes an amount or percentage of income to an employer-sponsored plan each pay period, like a 401(k), they are using the DCA method.

For example, let's use the following scenario: Someone makes $100,000 and they contribute 5% of their income to a 401(k) annually. The 5% amounts to $5,000 in this example. Let's say they get paid every other week; therefore, there are 26 pay periods (non-leap years). That boils down to $192.31 added to their 401(k) every other week.

When money is contributed in this manner, it is purchasing a chosen investment or multiple investments at a cost per share. Think of a cost per share like something you purchase at your local grocery store. For example, sometimes my favorite coffee is less than $5 because it's on sale, but most of the time it hovers around $7. Therefore, because the thought of not having coffee frightens me, I buy it almost every time I go to the grocery store. Inevitably, I'm buying it at different costs.

OK, so, here's the goal of the DCA strategy. Remember we said earlier that neither stock nor bond markets trend green every day. So, when investors add money consistently, there is a high probability that when contributions are made, the cost per share will be different each time. That is, it could be a higher or lower cost per share. Think back to my coffee example. Sure, I'd rather pay $5 per bag, but sometimes it costs $7. So, over the year, I might average $6 per bag, especially if I buy more when it's on sale.

Let's use average rate of return to better understand the DCA strategy. We used this example of average rate of return earlier:

$$5\% + 0\% + -2\% + 7\% + 7\% + 4\% + -1\% = 2.8\%$$

Now, we'll use similar numbers and say we purchased something at various costs of:

$$\$5 + \$2 + \$3 + \$7 + \$7 + \$4 + \$1 = \$4.14 \text{ is our average cost per share}$$

YOUR STRATEGY MATTERS (TO YOUR MONEY AND YOUR LIFE)

In this scenario, or while shopping, we're thankful when we can purchase items at a lower price because they are on sale. The difference, however, is that when I purchase my coffee, I'm accepting the fact that the money is never to be seen again; whereas investing is going toward a future value that I will be able to redeem later.

With this DCA scenario, the employee benefits from the opportunity of having the employer match their contribution (i.e., free money). In this scenario, the employee's 5% contribution could be greater when you factor in the employer's match of 3% or more. Now, instead of purchasing $5,000 in investments in a given year, the individual is purchasing $8,000—a reward of sorts, simply by applying the known best practice of investing.

And regarding matching, remember that free money also has the ability to compound. Why not try to double double the money that was contributed. Doubling the double looks like this:

$100,000 doubles to $200,000 (72/8 = 9) and
$200,000 folds into doubles to $400,000

This is an example of your gains, gaining more for you.

Know that matching, vesting, and other rules apply to all employer-sponsored plans. Getting into the weeds of the various plans is a completely different read. My suggestion is to know what is offered to you and to leverage it for your benefit. Information about this and other employer offerings should be included in your total benefits package; these benefits should be factored in when you consider salary or earning potential. Other benefits such as personal time off, hybrid work schedule, bonuses, and other perks should all be weighed carefully.

In short, the DCA strategy permits the account owner to purchase at different intervals with the goal of lowering the average cost per share. Think back to my favorite coffee. Hypothetically, if I could buy more of my favorite coffee at or around $5 and then sell it later at $7, because that's what the markets dictate, I win.

Application

The frequency in which you contribute to your accounts matters. The key question here is, what accounts are you consistently investing in?

The DCA method of investing is applicable to various aspects of our lives and should be something that we talk about more frequently. In our personal lives, our health routine could be seen as a parallel to the DCA investment method. Our exercise routine helps improve our average health and hopefully complements our eating, drinking, and sleeping routines. Better yet, to frequently invest in our four pillars is best. Even if it's a maintenance routine, some routine that is intentionally holding its ground is better than nothing. How consistent are you with your routines?

In my experience, there are many answers to this question, and they vary by season. My hope with this is to shed light on the fact that many of the routines in life are smaller in scale, but they offer large outcomes. For example, brushing your teeth takes two minutes, and it's recommended three times a day. Flossing is an added benefit, and in doing both regularly, you are investing in your physical health for the rest of your life. This is dental hygiene compounding, and it pays many dividends as you age. The same is true for many areas of our life.

Remember the TVM formula and the importance of compounding. It is often referred to as the Eighth Wonder of the World for a reason.

A word of encouragement: We all have our "shiny quarter" deterrents to best practices. Interestingly, shiny quarters only stay shiny as they are kept out of circulation, preserved, or polished. Here's what I've learned over the years, distractions lose credibility much quicker than our truly desired outcomes. Let's strive to keep our plans polished rather than sideline them.

Applying the DCA method to our personal lives can pay dividends for us and for others in our sphere of influence:
- Wouldn't it be refreshing to invest in others on their down days? Or have someone invest in us on our down days and celebrating with us on our up days?
- What's your vision for your marriage? Your children? Career? Health?
- And how are you routinely investing in these most valued relationships?

This is why planning is so important. Without planning we get distracted; we lose accountability, and we lose track. It's just the way it is in our world.

Remember that all forms of wealth have the potential to grow and double. Imagine the value of your various forms of wealth doubling over time. We'll talk about net worth later but for now, let your imagination go for a few minutes and visualize what that could look like. Next, let's talk about another common purchasing strategy known as buy and hold.

Buy and Hold
The second most commonly used investment strategy is called buy and hold. This strategy refers to the purchase of an asset, such as stocks, bonds, and real estate with the intent of keeping them over longer periods of time, regardless of short-term fluctuations. Makes sense, right? I mean, why invest in something that isn't going to benefit you over the long haul.

Here are a few key attributes of this investment strategy:
- Avoids market timing, aka attempting to predict market outcomes with the goal of preventing costly mistakes.
- Uses a diversified approach, which helps avoid duplication of effort or having concentrated investments in one or more categories.
- Reduces the tendency toward emotional buying and selling with the goal of avoiding costly mistakes.

Here are some pitfalls related to this strategy:
- It's important to make adjustments over time. It's wise to avoid the temptation to set it and forget it.
- Tax implications can get lost in this strategy.
- The purposes for investing will change over time, so it's important that strategy alignment is maintained and does not drift.

The buy and hold strategy tends to be more hands off than the DCA strategy. In other words, buy and hold is often referred to as more passive investing; hence the pitfalls mentioned above bear watching.

Application

The buy and hold strategy has its benefits; however, it's important not to confuse being passive with a lack of activity. Let's peel the onion back a layer or two. "Work smarter not harder" implies an action that is beneficial, more efficient, and potentially more profitable. It does not imply hands off, delegate it all, and put your feet up. The same is true of the statement, "Time is money," which is what this strategy seeks. Investors who use the buy and hold method want to invest in ways that delegate the heavy lifting of research and due diligence while investing in aspects that are less expensive and large-scale.

For investing and life, remember that we can be overly active and squeeze out margin, but we can also be overtly passive to our own detriment. Finding a healthy balance is the key. One of the aspects that I like about this strategy is the avoidance of trying to time the market.

> *For investing and life, remember that we can be overly active and squeeze out margin, but we can also be overtly passive to our own detriment. Finding a healthy balance is the key.*

Think back to the coffee example. When I see my favorite coffee on sale, I will often buy more than one bag. But I don't buy five bags because I've got other things to buy and because the freshness of coffee matters to me. So, on a grander scale, if I'm passive in what I know is best or if I don't leverage known best practices, I'm inadvertently choosing not to invest in what is best for my life. Why would I accept this depreciating thought? We wouldn't recommend that to our children, so why permit it in our lives?

Another known benefit of investing is the concept of diversification, which is a well-established best practice for investment portfolios. Diversification helps spread the potential for gains amongst different investments while also attempting to mitigate risk. Here's a quick visual: Think about snowshoes for a second. Snow and ice present several known difficulties, especially as they begin accumulating. However, the use of proper equipment mitigates some of these challenges and makes travel easier. The snowshoe helps keep the wearer on top of the snow, permitting a safer and more productive journey. How? A snowshoe increases the surface area and spreads the weight of the person out over a larger area. This is similar to how massive ships stay afloat with buoyancy. It's incredible that they can carry large amounts of weight and travel across oceans and through storms.

Investors who are ill-prepared will have a higher propensity to sink into the snowstorms of life known as distractions, comparison, and other forms of debt. Investing solely in ourselves, one stock, all cash, or solitude is a risky proposition; whereas gathering strengths, talents, experiences, and knowledge brings far better outcomes. Why bring a knife to a gun fight?

Regarding emotional buying or selling, our emotions are a gift—when we manage them well. Let's talk about investments requiring money. From the cars we drive, homes we live in, and the accounts we have, our emotions play a large part in our behaviors:

- We know that real estate is worth what someone else is willing to pay. Whether lower or higher, the market determines the purchase price, but the lender determines what they'll lend.
- The person selling a vehicle says it's in great condition and thinks they should get the retail price. But the dealership says the vehicle is in good condition, but it's worth less than you think.
- The investor says the markets are down, and so is my account. Why would I buy more? Yet the experienced investor knows the purpose is to lower the average cost per share and says buy, because the coffee is on sale for $4!

Now let's consider investments that don't have an exchange of money. First, remember that everything comes at a cost. Being passive may appear less costly, but without maintenance, passivity becomes very expensive:

- Your thought life should never be passive. Sure, rest is required, and chilling out can be healthy, but all too often, we can find ourselves in the passive zone.

- Regarding actions with ourselves and others near to us, with DCA-like routines, we may be better prepared to weather storms and ride the updrafts. Let's not be passive with the relationships we cherish most.

In my experience, the buy and hold strategy is best used in combination with DCA. I encourage you to continually evaluate your investing strategies, looking to invest while the chips are down, avoiding the fearmongers, and being rewarded for growth. With buy and hold, it is wise to establish a predetermined schedule for conversations such as quarterly reviews or family meetings to review life changes, strategy updates, changes in risk, and changes in purpose.

Day Trading
This strategy is exactly what it sounds like, the buying and selling of investments throughout the same day. In fact, by definition, this strategy states that no investments are held overnight. The goal in this strategy is to capitalize on market volatility and price fluctuations that occur with intraday trading.

This is a fast-paced environment and often requires a level of risk tolerance that is uncomfortable for many. Here's a quote from Forbes Advisor, "While day trading may seem exciting and lucrative it is effectively gambling with all the potential upsides and risks you'd have betting through any other avenue."[5]

Unlike DCA and buy and hold strategies, day trading does not value compounding; instead, it seeks gains by way of short-term transactions. This strategy is the instant gratification for investing; whereas the previous two are built for long-term purposes.

Here are some of the difficulties related to the day trading strategy:

- Taxes: Depending upon the account type, short-term gains might be applicable. These gains are treated as ordinary income instead of capital gains.
- Transaction fees: Because of the trade volume, increased fees can potentially erode profits.
- Risk: The risks related to this strategy are high, with estimates as high as 95% of day traders losing money.[6]
- Margin: One of the strategies common to this method is enhancing purchasing power with borrowed money, which means taking a loan to invest.

With challenges like these, you might ask, why this strategy is gaining popularity. Day trading offers the flexibility to work anywhere, known office hours, ease of starting, and the allure of high earnings. That's why it's attractive to some and the successes are highlighted on social media.

If someone has the means, a higher-than-average risk tolerance, and trusted research partners, then they might be willing to take this path with their own money. There is a reason, however, why institutional money, for the most part, is not managed with high volume trading like day trading.

Application

Just as DCA and buy and hold strategies have their attributes, the same is true of day trading. Here's what I appreciate about this approach. The ability to consistently decipher good and not so good on the fly is a helpful skill set. To have this skill set, manage cash reserves well, and consistently produce a profit is in essence a well-run business.

That said, day trading speaks to the uniqueness of being able to act and react on the fly and to consistently do so in a profitable manner. The best day traders have their strategies, and they don't deviate. They don't permit emotions in their decision-making, and they make quick decisions under stress. They are informed, and they utilize various resources.

In short, day traders have an orchestrated plan, an attribute, which is essential to most professions. The best coaches in football have a plan; they know their opponent and the health of their team; they know the environment, history, and coaching techniques; and they script the first several plays, if not the first few series of the game. The best businesses strive to do the same. And we can apply a similar approach to make our personal lives and homes just as productive.

Understand this and keep it close: Wise investing is a form of wealth as we invest in ourselves, others, and the future. This is a worthwhile process and less difficult for the person who understands that wealth comes in various forms.

Leadership

What investment strategies are you employing with your team(s)? Have you talked about growth and what that looks like for them and the organization? Have the "costs" related to productivity and slack been reviewed?

Consider the strengths on the team and how those work like diversification in a portfolio. Consider the three investment strategies and how they apply to career trajectories in your field. Engage in conversations that help your team see how the double the double benefits the clients, organization, and team. This is also a useful way to map our career paths.

THE TWO SIDES OF EVERY DOLLAR

Here are the **Wealth Coordinates** for this chapter.

Wealth instruments:
- Work toward growth while responsibly attending to different risk tolerances.
- Consistently seek out opportunities that wise people provide.
- See through the inconsistencies in the "get rich quick" overnight schemes designed to squander wealth.
- Respect the fact that time is required to improve inconsistencies in our actions and best thought-out plans.
- Understand that growth is an action that respects what we contribute.
- Comprehend the growth of growth and leverage it as often as possible.
- There is no slumber in their purposes, yet they rest comfortably.
- Are generous.
- Look after the best interests of others.
- Aways look at the potential and keep the long-term purposes front and center.

Debt instruments (e.g., doubt, fear, timidity, etc.):
- Are in no hurry (e.g., laziness and procrastination have no urgency)
- Don't seek resolution or improvement.
- What they lack in vision, they gain in consistent scarcity.
- Are not an ally, confidant, or protector. Yet they masquerade around as such.

- Quickly flee when needed for emotional or mental support.
- Are often more sticky than reflective.
- Do not rest.
- Do not benefit the beneficiary.
- Are not fiduciaries.
- Stare at shoelaces rather than gazing upon the horizon.

Benefitting no one yet asking that everyone participate, debt instruments, which exist all around us seek to divide us, keep us uneducated, uninformed, and in scarcity. Yet there is a solution.

Consider this thought: We, the most advanced species on the planet, struggle with the juxtaposition of accepting our behaviors that create positive outcomes while often deflecting the negative. The beautiful oak tree has no such thought or ability. It can however be grafted by another species known as the human.

If we don't like the reaping of what we sow thought, consider the reasoning:

- Are we disappointed in where we are? Who hasn't felt this at some point?
- Did we miss the mark or aspire to experience more? Yes. We have all missed the mark on something. Be glad that you aspire to more; that's a gift.
- Does it come from a place of judgment? Whose, yours or someone else's? If someone else casts judgment on you for something, I'm sorry that's happened. Truth is they've also failed and obviously, they failed to communicate well.

Who hasn't had these thoughts? Everyone is confronted with these at some point. Yet we can't graft our debt behaviors into wealth instruments. We can't be pessimists by default and think we are optimists. We can't constantly criticize and want to be known as encouragers. Our behaviors have patterns, and patterns produce outcomes.

I'm sorry if someone chose to share this message in an unhealthy manner. I'm sorry that life is difficult. I'm sorry that the noise is so prevalent. But please remember we inherited some of what we have. And yes, some of what we have is our own doing. But the potential that exists is within us and as we trust professionals and loved ones, we can advance toward a future that we can look back on and smile.

Knowing this and accepting it is what differentiates us from every other species on the planet. We can have thought experiments with ourselves and others contemplating the reasons to make shifts. We can choose to accept that we have been sowing a field that is exactly where we'd like to be, somewhere close or less desirable. We can make changes. Neuroplasticity is a real thing. We can consistently progress toward a life of significance, and this starts with accepting that we won't get it right all the time. No human ever has.

Sequence of Returns

Feelings are good servants but, they are disastrous masters.
—Dallas Willard

From an investment account perspective, sequence of returns is the order in which returns occur year after year in an investment account. Think back to the chapter on the Rule of 72. Here's the example that was used:

Yr 1 (5%) + Yr 2 (0%) + Yr 3 (–2%) + Yr 4 (7%) + Yr 5 (7%) + Yr 6 (4%) + Yr 7 (–1%)

In this scenario, the sequence of returns is 5%, then 0%, then –2%, and so on. Sequence of returns is the account performance annually in successive years. When we average the years, we get the average rate of return over a specified period. In this case, seven years. For example, with these years, we see an average rate of return of:

5% + 0% + –2% + 7% + 7% + 4% + –1% = 2.86%

From an investment account perspective, here are a few reasons why sequence of returns matters:

- There is a risk associated with sequence of returns known as, you guessed it, sequence of returns risk. This is the risk that investment account values experience a decline during one or more of the following seasons: when someone is approaching retirement, shortly after someone retires, and late in life.
- Why do these seasons matter more than others? Because if retirement accounts experience a considerable decline in value, let's say −8%, and an income is being withdrawn from the account at, let's say 3%, then account values experience a total decline of 11% from both events. And that's without accounting for inflation.
- Finally, to withdraw cash for income from an investment account, an exchange is required. For example, cash is received from dividends, yield, the sale of investments, or similar exchanges. This matters because during poor market years, if withdrawals for income stay the same, it's possible that more investments would need to be sold to provide the same income. Just like the income you earned for work during your career, your investments are working to provide income and growth throughout retirement. There are, however, no sick days, PTO, or vacations.

No one wants to be concerned about income during their working years, and the same is true during retirement. But many households do worry about the transition because change is difficult to grasp. However, as a reminder, the sequence of our thought life improves with preparation, much like our sequence of returns. Let's unpack this.

Our working years are synonymous with what we call the accumulation phase of life. This is when our career produces an income that then goes toward our household 5Us. This season often lasts anywhere from four to six decades.

We then transition to what is called the distribution phase of life, most commonly referred to as retirement. Personally, I like to refer to this as a transition to a life of significance. This phase lasts until we pass away, and during this time, our retirement savings work for us, producing income that goes toward our household 5Us. A lot happens during this transition, which is why we encourage clients to practice retirement during the three to five years prior to the actual date.

It is wise to be aware of and prepared for the various forms of risk related to this transition. A few common retirement strategies help with these risks, and I encourage you to learn which philosophy works best for your plan. At our office, we prefer to counter this risk with what is called the Bucket Strategy. Others prefer to use the 4% Rule we spoke of earlier. Some choose products to build layers of income.

My goal in sharing this is to raise awareness and to combat concern with preparedness. As we all know, it's not the green up and to the right days that create concern; it's the red and down days that alter the sequence of our thought lives and returns.

Let's switch gears . . . Some aspects of our lives will always be beyond our control. Accepting this truth should immediately relieve tension within us and others. However, some aspects of our lives are within our control, starting with the way we prepare, live, and handle life. We also have the option of knowing possible outcomes and being realistic about probabilities.

It helps to start with understanding how our emotions and feelings play a role in our circumstances. I like to think of emotions as the script or play written (conscious or subconscious) and feelings as the actors or actresses entertaining the audience (reacting to an emotion, portraying a physical portrait of a mental event).

Interestingly, with more awareness of this phenomenon using emotional intelligence (EQ), we can reason with ourselves to prevent our feelings from becoming disastrous masters as Dallas Willard noted. Unfortunately, the opposite is true too. We can make matters worse just as quickly.

We can enhance the superhighways of our thought life and help guide our way around the "disastrous" aspects of our emotions through neuroplasticity. Contrary to the saying, "you can't teach an old dog new tricks," we humans can learn new things. Neuroplasticity is basically the brain's ability to change and adapt much like our GPS does when it informs us that a new route is available to avoid a slowdown ahead. And much like on our GPS, when it asks whether we want to accept this alternate path, we either accept or decline. Change is sometimes difficult, but it is available.

The sequence of your thought life matters. When you were growing up, how did you learn? I knew I liked the social aspect of high school and college; therefore, if I showed up to class and took notes, that cut down on my study time. The combination of those two actions helped cement my learning and memorization, and therefore helped with my testing. As a bonus, I got my social time.

This is an example of how planning can work. Some don't like planning because they think they miss out on things they enjoy. That's not necessarily true. Much like I enjoyed hanging out with others at school, I always remembered why I was there (purpose) and that was to get educated, graduate, and then get a job. Second, I knew that to keep my truck, I had to maintain the grades for a 2.5 GPA mandated by my parents. Finally, to graduate I knew it was best for me to go to class and take notes. To this day I am still a notetaker.

Your experiences are important, and it is helpful to know what part of learning you enjoy most. It's equally important to know your reward system and for you to share that with those closest to you. This is similar to knowing our love language.

A possible solution to some of life's speed bumps is retooling knee-jerk reactions by applying the way we learn. This is part of our thought life. For example, think back to how you answered the question about your earliest memory of money. In some way, your earliest memories shaped your fiscal behavior—good, bad, or indifferent.

In the chapter on wealth, debt, and beneficiaries, we touched on some of the more common debt instruments such as fear and doubt. Now, let's throw in some negative claims related to those debt instruments to see how our thought life works. Over the years, I've used and heard many different claims such as:

> "Not again . . ."
> "What now?"
> "Really? Now, come on."
> "That's not for me."
> "Nah, I'm good. I don't need any help."
> "Tried it . . . not for me."
> "I'm not good at . . ."
> "I'll never be . . ."
> "That's not how I'm wired."
> "No one cares."
> "I'm so stupid . . ."

Quick truth statement: If more negative than positive is being spun in your thought life, maybe you should pull off the road, listen, and insert some what-ifs. What if God is trying to protect, bless, or encourage you? Or what if someone who loves you is trying to tell you something? Or what if your subconscious is speaking to your conscious and begging you to stop? The sequence of your thought life matters to all the ways you qualitatively and quantitatively view life, including your 5Us.

Everyone knows that being strapped with debt is unproductive and costly. OK, well, so is consistently telling yourself negative thoughts or speaking negatively over others. There is no benefit to anyone in this equation. Plus, as this pattern continues, mental and emotional interest is being accrued just like it does on credit cards. And everyone within earshot or proximity is affected negatively. No one benefits.

Instead of asking "Why me?" or "What now?" or worse, try a different approach and ask yourself what's in it for me (WIFM). To invest in yourself isn't selfish; it's one of the best fiduciary actions any one of us can take. I like the question: "What am I being invited into?" Recurring themes, both good and bad, don't just happen. If you're consistently seeing something you dislike, invest in some due diligence and find out what's creating the issues. That's the same process that the person who consistently sees progress is doing; they're just asking questions from a different perspective. Their questions are more like, "What's working well?" or "What else do I need to change?" Some people see setbacks as data or information, and they want to learn from it. Others see setbacks as a reason not to keep going. Our emotions, words, actions, and thoughts play a role on both sides; neuroplasticity helps either way.

Let's switch gears. When was the last time you allowed your imagination to run free? Maybe growing up you dreamed of being a doctor, astronaut, athlete, firefighter, or another profession. Maybe you dreamed recently of opening your own business, retiring, or taking a trip. Whatever it was or whatever you are dreaming of now, the use of your imagination is a gift.

Do you recall as a child imagining the monster in the closet or under the bed, especially after watching scary movies or as the wind blew limbs that scraped the house? As children, we used our imagination freely. As adults, we still imagine the monster in the closet or under the bed except the monsters have taken on different names, such as shame, approval, vanity, fear, doubt, anxious thoughts, negative thoughts, unwarranted noise, and other life-draining debt instruments that still immobilize us like the make-believe creature under our bed. Eric Church's song "Monsters" provides a good reminder for us. Learning to use the gift of our imagination to combat our "monsters" requires awareness and practice; whereas allowing our imagination to immobilize us takes less effort, so it is easier to lean this direction. And this will impact your 5Us. Your thought life matters.

It's been said that each is given according to their ability. I want you to know that you are already approved and that your abilities are gifts in waiting. I ask that you reflect on the various forms of wealth that you already possess. Receive this, please.

Wealth Coordinate: The difference between the wildly successful and those who aspire to be wildly successful is often one relationship away. You are the relationship that is one relationship away, and you have it within you to make a difference in the mirror as well as within others you care about.

The sequence of your thought life is quite possibly the most important aspect of your life. As your thought life goes, so goes the rest of your life. There is a reason why highly compensated professionals pay for advisors and coaches that help them see past themselves.

Application

Which thought life do you promote most? Do you mostly promote a thought life that invests in your future growth like the two men in the parable of the talents who doubled the amounts they were given. Or is your thought life one that buries your potential, like the third man in the parable? Here are a few mind hacks that will improve your thought life and outcomes:

- Seek wisdom and understanding and develop routines that promote wellness. One of my go-to reads is James 1:5 which says, *"If you need wisdom, ask our generous God, and He will give it to you. He will not rebuke you for asking."*
- Work toward something rather than nothing. We are each uniquely positioned for something, and our experience matters. Oftentimes, blessings, better circumstances, and upward trends are waiting for us when we take action. If we are waiting for change to proceed, that will often present a new set of struggles as idleness rarely promotes health. The one who says, "Well, I'd work harder if they paid me more" or "I'd tithe if I made more" will more than likely not see a higher income.
- With good intentions and effort, positive outcomes are more likely to come. However, no matter how good an intention is, without effort, it is simply a thought. It's much like getting into a car but not starting the engine. When deciding on a direction, consider whether you are aiming toward something that you'll want to return to.

    If you were able to step outside of yourself and review your life from a different perspective, how would you feel about the action you are pondering? What is your first thought? If the thought is unproductive, it is possible that it needs to be tweaked or replaced.

- Caution and nerves are your allies and often your armor bearers. Unhealthy fear and doubt are not your friends, protectors, or allies; they are your enemy. Regarding fear, I'm not referring to an awareness of danger, awe, or "Spider" sense; these are gifts, and we should pay close attention to them. Instead, the fear I have in mind is speculation of failure above promise, perfectionism or traditionalism over tradition, or fear of change that pushes one toward complacency. This kind of fear is a debt instrument that stalls growth and will not help on your journey.
- Choose carefully who you listen to. Your scouts will either promote or not promote health within your life. The best athletes, the best performers, the best organizational leaders understand the value of a healthy respect for opportunities, and they address the nerves with preparation, optimism, teamwork, and other helpful resources. Think of the butterflies in your stomach as a healthy respect for what lies before you and proceed with a cautiously optimistic attitude.
- Who is on your team? You were not meant to do this alone, and you don't have to. The sooner we get away from the thought that we are alone in this life, the better. We, not me, will go further; the concept of "we" is more sustainable.
- A word of caution: No matter how deep the mud is, when you are stuck, you're stuck, and the only way out is another truck with a chain or wench. Phone a friend, trust someone, meet with a professional, and get out of the mud. There is no shame in this!

Leadership

How are you investing into your emotional intelligence (EQ) and your team's EQ? The sequence of our thought life as leaders begets the health of others. The old school "do as I say, not as I do" leadership technique is thankfully fading as today's productivity is more often spurred on with authenticity and genuineness.

Are you including the five components of EQ in conversations and reviews? Those five components are self-awareness, self-regulation, motivation, empathy, and social skills. Is it possible to illustrate a Time Value of EQ (TVEQ) while charting potential productivity? Have you evaluated and measured your meetings for transparency, accuracy, and creativity? Are these encouraged and if possible, incentivized or rewarded?

Consider these and ask others to join you. Today's multigenerational workforce is more open to and thirsting for involvement than some think. It's great to see how many people want to work for an organization that they believe in, especially as organizations reciprocate belief in their teams. Invest in yourself. Invest in your thought life.

Growth

Growth is more often gradual than instant. Growth occurs at different ages, in different styles, with various opportunities and if that wasn't enough, it's different for each of us.

Growth in my profession often takes on two overlapping yet different paths, which often converge at some point to create an enjoyable season. The type of growth discussed most in my profession is the compounding growth of an investment account. It's the upward and to the right, green percentage that we should see in our accounts over time. Growth does not happen every year, and it's possible that for two or sometimes three consecutive years, growth might not occur. However, if we follow a plan, we should expect growth in our investment accounts over time.

The other growth that we reference, though it is observed less in my industry, is growth within ourselves. This qualitative growth is more difficult to measure because it isn't measured in dollars or percentages. Like our first memory of money, qualitative growth has a deeply personal origin. And as I'm sure you've noticed, I care deeply about this growth. In fact, I think this qualitative growth (G1) begets the other (G2), quantitative growth.

In the parable of the talents, we are told that two of the men invested the money with which they were entrusted, and they doubled the original amount, earning G2 growth. One important aspect that wasn't provided in the parable is the length of time all three men held the original investment; it may have been a long time. So, let's hypothetically use a longer timeframe such as forty years, before the money was needed or accounted:

WI (Wealth Instrument) x Risk x Time = Projected Growth

What wealth instruments do you have in your possession? We talked about these in the "Wealth, Debt, and Beneficiaries" chapter. Consider that one of your wealth instruments could very well be the G1 growth you've experienced. That is, the qualitative growth you've seen in yourself and have been able to share with others. Sure, it's much easier to review the growth of your investment accounts (G2), but you also have other forms of wealth.

To help review both G1 and G2, let's start with the easier of the two, your investment accounts. Are you experiencing growth that's on the path of the two men in the parable who doubled their original amounts? If not, that doesn't automatically mean something is wrong. Let's consider the purpose of the account:

- If the funds in the account are not needed for a long time, it should be expected to grow (purpose). Using the average rate of return and R72, you can project when you should double the amount with two exceptions:
  - » Wait until the account has been in place for 12 months before using your own R72.
  - » If the account was created in a poor performing market year, you will need to wait until green percentages are added to the averages.

- If the purpose of the account is preservation, then doubling the amount is not the desired outcome. For example, if a teenager is two years away from entering college and a college account is going to help fund their education, then in many cases, higher risk (growth) has been taken off the table and replaced with preservation because the purpose has changed from growth to paying for college.
- If the purpose is income, say for a retired couple, then some of the assets should be set aside for income and, therefore, not expecting to double; other assets are seeking growth because the plan is to keep a steady income for the next thirty years. In short, this is the Bucket Strategy approach.

A final word about the man in the parable who buried the investment he was given. Notice that he didn't seek any interest from a bank. As you may recall from our discussion of simple interest, cash sitting in the bank earns something. At a minimum, it's in preservation mode and countering some of the diminishing effects of inflation. Plus, it's not likely to be stolen and most likely FDIC-insured. Last I checked, burying anything in the ground is worse unless we're talking about a luau. I'm in for that.

For what it's worth, note that there is no fourth man in the parable who spent it all or fifth man who spent it all and took on debt.

Growth is a marvel that is often hard to understand. However, it is not hard to understand that we can't grow what we don't have; we can't grow what we owe to others, and we can't grow what we squander. And that's how I interpret the parable of the talents. The message is much like that of the Twisted Sister video of my youth: "What are you going to do with your life?!" That's moral of the parable: What are you doing with the talents and strengths you have or have been given?

Earlier I said that growth has an origin. How were G1 growth and learning instilled during your childhood? For some it was conditional, and in my experience, that's not always a bad thing. For example, as you know, I had to get a 2.5 GPA to keep my truck in college and that requirement helped me. It set a benchmark for me, and I was rewarded for accomplishing the goal.

For others maybe G1 growth and learning were demonstrated and encouraged through healthy conversations. Unfortunately, for some, threats were used, or expectations were held over their heads. Either way, just as your first memory of money and what you learned growing up set monetary wheels in motion, your views on growth were initially formed in the same way. I know people who will never touch alcohol because of what they saw in a parent. I know people who will never live on a farm because the thought of milking another cow wakes them up at four in the morning. I know others who won't move back to a small town or who won't move out of the small town because of past experiences. My point is this: To learn how to get to where you want to go, you must first know where you're starting from. Along the way, you get to decide what you want to bring with you and what you want to drop off at the train station; you can make changes.

Switching gears: Do you think the man in the parable who was given two bags was envious of the one who was given five bags? Or what about the man who was given one bag? What do you think he thought about the other two men whom he quite possibly knew? Is this potential difference in thought life a G1 growth opportunity that we could incorporate in our own lives?

How envious of others are you? How often do you window shop, comparing yourself to others? How often do you tell others how much better your life is on some social platform? Of course, we are already aware that no one is perfect and that most displays on social media are of the filtered, edited, and best of the multiple attempts variety. For the most part, we also know that if it has to be said on such a public platform, maybe the person who needs convincing is the person taking the selfie.

Getting past the hang-ups that keep pulling us backward instead of building us up is difficult. The good news is the sequence of your thought life plays a key role. This along with your purpose, team, and plan makes a world of difference. This does not imply that struggles cease to exist for the prepared. However, who do you feel is more likely to consistently experience better outcomes in life's ups and downs, the prepared or ill-prepared?

If you were giving one, two, or five bags of money to someone to invest for you, I'm quite certain that you would conduct an evaluation of talent and exercise due diligence. And more than likely, your decision would match the recipients' abilities. Not only is life not a DIY project, it's also not a selfie.

We are gravitating toward a life of loneliness, and we have permitted creep to dissolve what we value most. As a reminder, COVID-19 helped us see what we value most as distance and isolation kept us away from the people we love and activities we enjoy. If we're not careful, we will gravitate away from what we learned and back to what we had. Like the former lottery winner who won the opportunity to live a life that was different, only to squander it.

A life of self-sufficiency is not sustainable. I appreciate how Arnold Schwarzenegger said it, "I am not a self-made man,"[7] and in his book, he takes the time to reference dozens who helped him in his journey.

Application

Growth is a long-term journey. The markets will fluctuate, as will your life, and over time, our TVMs will reflect the consistency of our investments in G1 and G2 growth. This will affect our sequence of returns, average rate of returns, and personal ROI using the Rule of 72. How are you investing in your future?

I encourage you to permit yourself to experience the journey, knowing that fluctuation and volatility are going to occur. The bumper sticker was correct: "Stuff happens." However, if you are going to buy low and sell high for investing in accounts, then do it across the board. Invest in the low times. Learn from mistakes. Invest in wealth instruments like forgiveness, trust, empathy, and the like. Bolster routines that improve investing in more than money and rates of return.

I make this promise to you: Consistently investing in the things that matter most to you will by far exceed the opposite. I further make this promise: Investing in the qualitative aspects of your life helps you see what contentment means. If you really want to know you've arrived somewhere, know what it means to have enough.

The persistent, hardworking, and driven person with a purpose, team, and plan is consistently a proof of concept. Discipline turns into fulfilment, eventually. When you see the person consistently giving their all at home, work, or the gym, be assured that they have reached the point that feels rewarding. At the risk of sounding countercultural, it is liberating to know that we don't have to know it all and that others can be trusted to help us reach our fullest potential.

Leadership

Leaders, how are you instilling growth and development in your team(s)? Remember that it's not just about the G2 growth of numbers. Investing in your team's G1 growth will create several other helpful attributes that you will have the opportunity to review in time. For example, as morale and culture develop, you can create a way to monitor momentum. As mission loss improves, you can develop ways to monitor productivity. Get creative with offering incentives. Get to know how each of your team members feels rewarded. Also important to planning, when you're hitting on all cylinders, be mindful of what created the altitude and what will keep it. It's one thing to know how to get to a healthy cruising altitude. It's another to maintain it or to know how to land the plane.

Communication

Have you ever wondered about the origin of words and what brought them about? Sometimes, words spring up overnight. Take for example, *social distancing*. It was the newest phrase added in 2020; prior to that year, I don't recall hearing or ever using it.

Some words have gravitated away from their original intent toward a negative connotation even though the original definition was not negative. For example, the word *content* was used just a couple of paragraphs back; it's strange how a positive word is now used to imply settling. What about *discipline, profit, delayed gratification, sacrifice, correction*, and *accountability*?

Also note how, especially in the English language, many words have dual meanings. And now, despite the risk of sounding old, words are being replaced with emojis and GIFs. All this to say that our word choice, frequency, and way we communicate with others is crucial to our growth together. Our communication is arguably one of the most important aspects of our lives and that is our **Wealth Coordinate** for this chapter.

I've said it before, and I stand firm on the fact that money is not one of the primary reasons for divorce. In the same respect, money is not the root problem that leads to health concerns such as heart disease, stroke, or diabetes.

Money is not a living or breathing creation; it does not have the authority to create these things that are a part of our culture. Let me communicate this as clearly as I know how: Money is a valuable resource. It is an instrument, tool, barometer, resource, which is available to us. It is very helpful in:

- Our day-to-day activities as we consume (5U of spending)
- Our generosity as we aspire to invest in matters that are important to us by giving to others or organizations (5U of generosity)
- Our plans for the future (5U of investing)
- Activities we enjoy (5U of spending)

Let me drive the point home as to why money isn't the issue. If you flip the script and look at successful marriages, thriving businesses, healthy emotions, strong mental gains, happiness, joy, peace, love, and rest, do we hear people giving money credit for these? No.

Sure, capital is useful in business. But a thriving business credits its people, vision, planning, and execution. Sure, money can buy a boat. I know because I've bought one. I also know the phrase often heard among boat owners: "The two happiest days of boat ownership are the day you bought it and the day you sold it."

Sometimes, it appears that those who have a lot of money are happy. But the ones who speak about it and how much things cost are often lonely. I hope this repetition helps retool the thoughts that have permeated our homes, businesses, and organizations. Money doesn't have the authority to either discourage or create issues. It is our perspective, behaviors, management, consumption, and investing of money that promote abundance or create issues. Loving money more than our most valued things is when we start seeing it being blamed . . . interesting how that works.

That's why our communication with ourselves and others matters. Reflect on the truth statement that both wealth and debt come in various forms. Do you know someone who often demonstrates a propensity that trends up and to the right and it often seems that everything they do turns to gold? First, that person is not perfect. In large part, their success comes from knowing the importance of surrounding themselves with others who are more intelligent and more successful. They are comfortable in their own skin, and they desire the pursuit of bringing value to something bigger than themselves. Finally, they understand what negative speech, talking down to others and themselves, and constant criticism of others and themselves does.

That's called an abundance mentality, and it starts with what we think of ourselves, our worth, our purpose, and the value we bring to others. And each of these boils down to how we communicate with ourselves. This then improves our ability to speak with others. It's time to take the authority back!

Before we proceed, please know that I do not define abundance as riches of money, fame, and stuff. These aren't wrong, but in themselves, they aren't what create an enjoyable, peace-filled, joyful, sustainable life. OK, let's move.

You take the authority back by first knowing where the authority comes from. From there, with purposeful communication and planning, you build upon your purpose, plans, and hopes for your future. We'll talk more about planning in the "Planning" chapter later in this book. For now, let's look at some communication applications:

- **Parents:** Talk about money with your kiddos more frequently. Share the positives and the negatives. There's no need for specifics early on; however, as they get older, age-specific discussions will be helpful. Talk about the five uses of money: giving, saving, spending, debt, and taxes. Then, take it to the next level; talk about your mistakes. That amplifies the learning and creates an even greater communication bridge for your relationship and a brighter trajectory for your children. Our children are much more capable and resilient than we give them credit for. Relate to the stuff that matters to them (e.g., new toy, new game, device, friends). When we relate to their WIFM (What's In It For Me), the impact goes much further.
- **Spouses:** Set time aside routinely on a schedule that fits best for you both. Find a great brunch spot and talk. Find a park. Sit informally in the living room. Wherever it is, talk frequently about what you value most, such as how things are going, the future, trips, children, home. Don't expect that both of you will be on the same page, but know that when you communicate effectively, you don't have to over-communicate. If one is more geared than the other toward a particular topic, be empathetic and lean in. You are investing in your marriage and other aspects of your life together. This is not a business meeting; these meetings should be informal, subject to change, and fluid. Finally, don't start with the negatives or what needs improvement all the time. No one likes reviews of what they're doing wrong all the time. Grow the quality of your EQ and just hang out together. Talk. Care about each other and the bigger picture.

- **Friends:** It appears everyone is an expert these days; yet it's hard to find the person who reads, listens, or attends without criticism. Experts observe, listen, lean in, and ask good questions. They don't immediately go for the, "Well, you know . . ." Life doesn't grow, "Well, you know . . ." without good soil, sun, and water. Share each other's burdens without judgment. Listen to others in need. And, if you say you are going to do something, please do it.

One of my personal favorites is our propensity to speak louder when communication begins to break down. Don't you love it when we automatically start speaking louder on the phone when people can't hear us on the other end? As if it's a distance problem. Or what about when one speaks a different language and the other person seems to think that the solution is to speak louder and slower? It doesn't work at my favorite Mexican restaurant, at home, in business, or anywhere else. Let's find a better way that benefits both parties.

I can't emphasize this enough: If something is important to you personally or professionally, measure it. There is nothing wrong with talking about what you value most and then determining how to track whether you're making progress. With good conversation that focuses on the mutually beneficial aspect, you can learn how to effectively communicate your hopes, dreams, and fears and then measure whether you are tracking toward progress.

If you don't do something now, don't expect it to spring up overnight. The good ole New Year's resolution pattern of failure helps further justify the need to effectively progress toward best practices like communication. If you're not doing something now and expect that you're going to gain the ability to drastically change during your sleeping hours, unfortunately that plan has a high probability of failure. We don't live in *The Matrix*, and we can't plug into something and become great at it just because we had one experience with it. Instead, take the bigger picture and break it down into bite-size pieces. If you haven't read *12-Week Year* by Brian P. Moran and Michael Lennington or *Atomic Habits* by James Clear, pick these up. Both will serve you well in your personal and professional life.

Effective communication is the lynchpin to most of the potential outcomes we have in life. When we don't communicate effectively, the reverse is also true. We must get better at communicating with ourselves and others. This is crucial for our existence together. And when we improve this critical aspect of life, we will make advancements toward healthier mental and emotional communities. And our collective 5Us will improve as well.

Exchange Rates

When you eat or drink, what do you gain from the exchange? Take food, for example. Hopefully, when you enjoy a new dish, your favorite food, or your favorite restaurant, you receive some nourishment and many other benefits in exchange. For instance, you might experience time well spent with others, peace and quiet, satisfying taste, old and new memories and experiences, and other benefits. Drink is similar. Water, for example, or here in the South, sweet tea offers hydration. Coffee is mostly water, but as I remind my dad, the caffeine in coffee may negate the benefits of hydration. Ask me if that works when we meet . . .

In my profession, exchange rates are related to currency that either comes into the US or exits. If you've traveled to other countries, you've most likely experienced some form of currency exchange in which you received a value that is less than, more than, or equal to the currency you had.

For example, in 2023 the average exchange rate for the Canadian (CAD) dollar to the US dollar was .7408 USD. Here's an illustration provided by Exchange Rates UK:

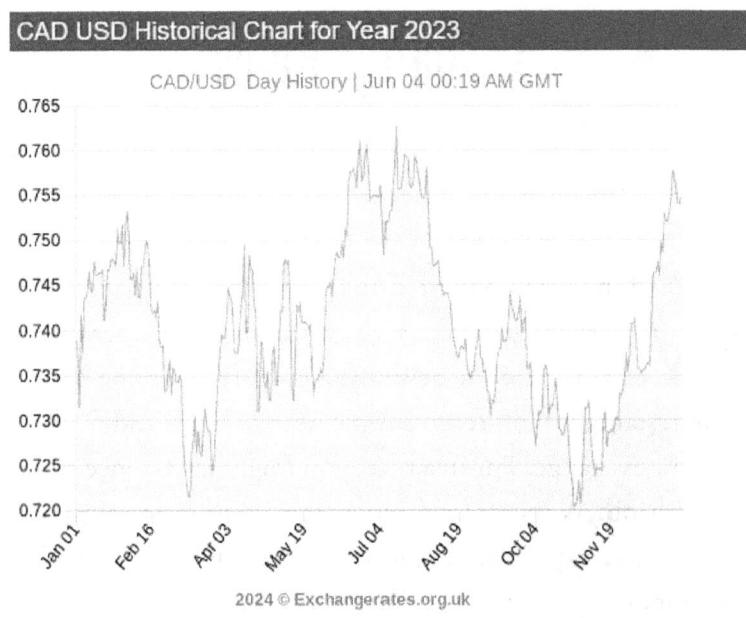

From this graph, you see that the lowest CAD exchange rate was on October 28th, and that was .7204 USD. Conversely, the highest exchange rate was on July 13th, and that was .7628 USD. So, if I had one CAD dollar, I would get roughly 75% of the value back to me in USD.

For comparison, let's review the other direction. The average exchange rate for US dollar to the Canadian dollar in 2023 was 1.3501 CAD. Here's an illustration provided by Exchange Rates UK:

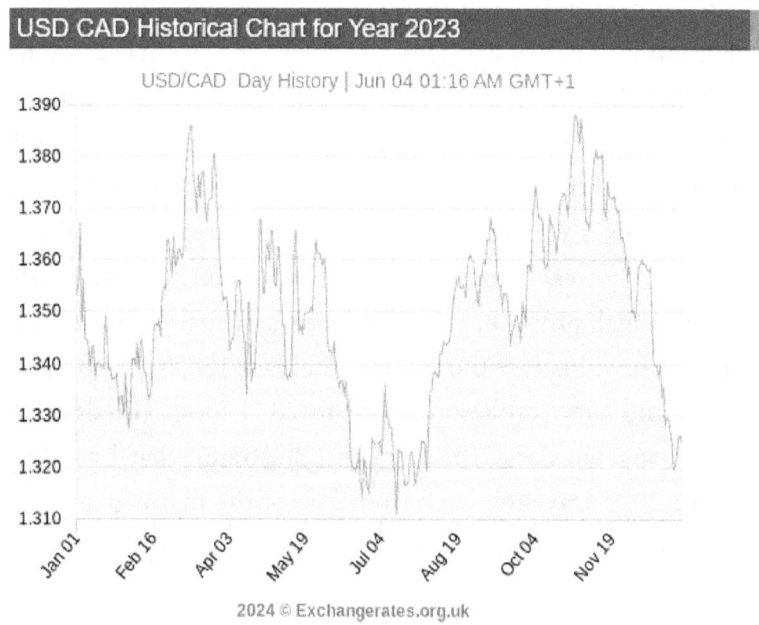

This graph shows that the lowest exchange rate occurred on July 13th at 1.311 CAD, and the highest exchange rate occurred on October 28th at 1.3881 CAD.

Notice the differences in the graphs. First, if I had traveled from where I live in the US to one of the many beautiful spots in Canada and exchanged US currency, I would have gotten roughly $1.35 Canadian dollars for every US dollar.

Notice anything else? Look at the peaks and valleys and the overlap, using the dates to help. There's a relationship in the exchange as one currency goes down and the other goes up. The highest exchange rate for one becomes the lowest for the other and vice versa. From a macro perspective, exchange rates fluctuate as the value of one currency increases or decreases in relationship to the other. Behind this lies a whole world of macro and microeconomics in which others far smarter than me work and live.

For our purposes, my intent is to shed light on what an exchange rate looks like—how it relates to our patterns and routines—and to illustrate how our strengths and weaknesses impact both ourselves and those around us. As we gain a clearer understanding of the exchanges we experience daily, we can begin to make more intentional choices. These choices, in turn, can lead to improved fiscal, relational, physical, emotional, and spiritual exchange rates.

To further illustrate the thought, here are the exchange rates for the USD and Mexican Peso (MXN) in 2023. Both visuals are from www.exchangerates.org. The first chart illustrates what I would have gotten in 2023 traveling back from one of the many great spots in Mexico to where I live in the US.

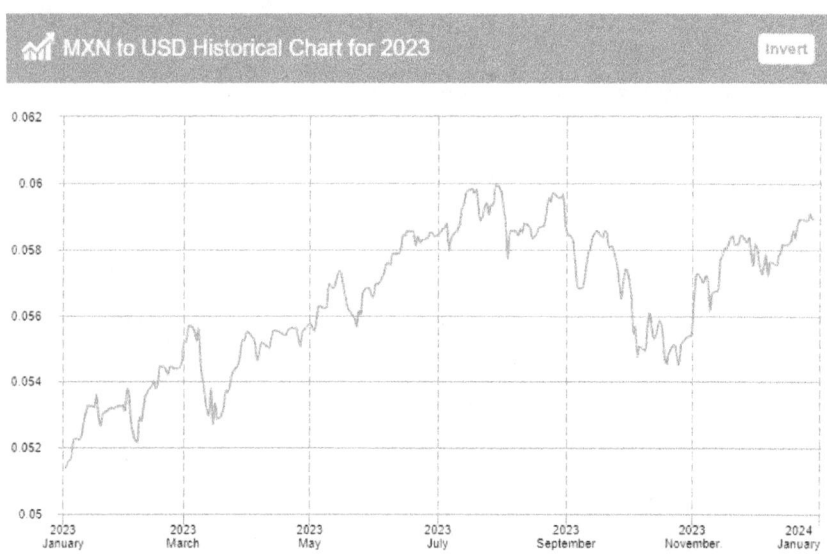

The highest exchange rate was .05992 USD on July 28th, the average for the year was .05646, and the lowest was .05138 USD on January 2nd.

This next chart shows what I would have gotten in exchange for one USD in MXN Peso traveling to Mexico in 2023.

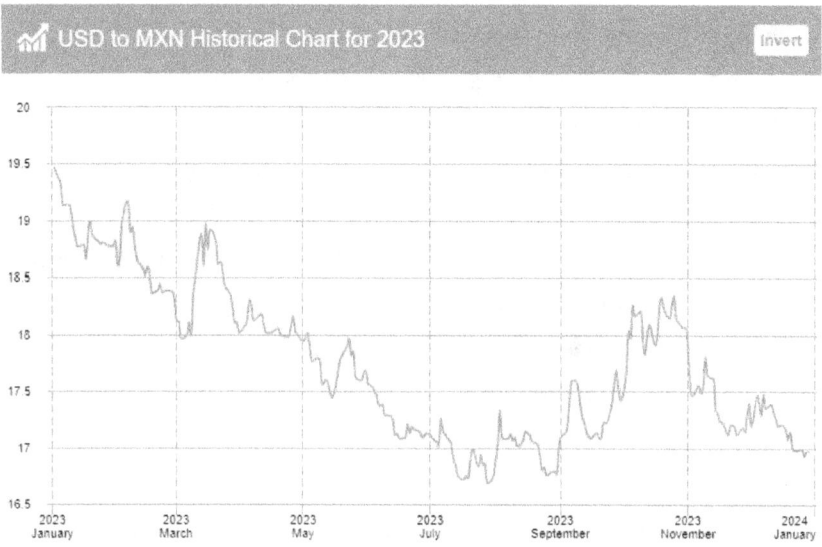

The highest rate was 19.463 MXN on January 2nd, the average for the year was 17.738, and the lowest was 16.690 MXN on July 28th.

I like these two illustrations for a couple reasons. First, I'm a visual learner, and data helps me see things. For example, notice that in October 2023, all three currencies experienced some volatility. Similarly, in January and July 2023, these currencies also experienced some volatility as the strength of one currency gained or declined in value.

Second, I like visuals like these because they help me visualize important parallels. For example, think back to our discussion of food and drink exchange at the beginning of this chapter. Two of our basic needs are met with the exchange of money: Food alleviates hunger and provides nourishment and energy while water quenches thirst and sustains life. If you were to graph these exchanges like we do for currency, would there be some similarities in the high, low, and average figures of value-to-cost exchange or health-to-cost exchange? I know there would be for me.

Now let's think about another basic need for life, shelter. An exchange is made for shelter as a home is purchased, mortgaged, or rented. How much would you pay for a good night's sleep? That represents another exchange for physiological need.

What about clothing? How much of your annual spend is exchanged on this basic need? From a physiological perspective, the other basic need for life is air. Thankfully, for the most part, this is not something we have to reach into our pockets for; however, we are responsible for maintaining and improving our air quality. And let's not forget there are many who for one reason or another are unable to provide food, water, clothing, or shelter for themselves.

The life-sustaining attributes of food and water have long been referenced in parables and metaphors to parallel the benefits of healthy behaviors. Interestingly, the nourishment, calories, carbs, fat, and waste we receive from the food we consume each serve the body differently as nutrients, energy or waste is processed. Also interesting, ever noticed being tired after lunch?

What we ingest, physically and mentally, does not necessarily provide nourishment and, therefore, implies that some of the exchange of our time and hard-earned income is the consumption of waste. Worse yet, over extended periods of time, higher exchanges of income for waste will inhibit our body's ability to convert energy and nutrients efficiently. You might also be surprised by the effects of stress on our metabolism and how it's often what we promote or permit that taxes our metabolism more than aging.

I'm not going down the don't-do-this-or-that path; I like my food and drink just as much as the next. However, in my fifty-plus years, I have learned a lot more about what my intake does to my body, and I'm thankful for the awareness even though it came from unhealthy exchanges.

Another exchange that matters is income earned in exchange for work provided. I remember reading a 2019 Gallup report that said, "Less than 50% of U.S. workers feel that they are in good jobs."[8] Yet, work-life balance is generally cited and supported like it's the greatest thing since sliced bread. I couldn't disagree more and here's why. The fact that the word *work* comes before *life* in this phrase says it all. The correct sequence is *life-work* balance. To keep using the phrase *work-life* has the same impact as saying work-family balance or work-health balance. When priorities are out of tilt, a decline in enjoyment follows. This isn't an earth-shattering public safety announcement, but most of us have experienced this negative flow in our work-life imbalance.

It's time we paid more attention to our personal data and why it exists. When someone enjoys their evenings, weekends, holidays, and vacations, and work doesn't infringe on their joy in their personal life, work will likely be more productive. The sooner we respect that a person isn't alive primarily to produce blood, sweat, and tears for their employer, the sooner we'll see improved satisfaction data as well as the productivity that organizations seek.

Work is a normal part of life—and for most of us, it's necessary. Sometimes it takes priority, like during a big career move, when unexpected bills come up, or when extra income is needed for school or travel. And some employees don't see their work as a job because of how enjoyable it is. We should be mindful of our priorities and create healthy boundaries that alert us when shifts in priorities occur. Otherwise, lifestyle creep has the tendency to promote an unhealthy exchange in life and the things we value most.

Applications

Income — In exchange for the requirements of the work you provide, are you supporting the quality of life that you want? Consider the commute, hours, environment, evenings, weekends, and stress that comes with your role. I am by no means suggesting that stress shouldn't come with the role or that long hours and responsibilities aren't required. Work is work and with that, there are various levels of both stress and time. Given what you provide to your employer and clients, is the exchange of your time, energy, brain power, physical effort, culture aptitude, results, commute, and work ethic worth the compensation you receive?

Do your values drive your 5Us, or is it the other way around? What does this exchange look like? Is it complementary or conflicting?

Another word of caution about how you look at income. Providing for a family requires a variety of wealth instruments. Provision doesn't only come in the form of money. Consider this, if parents desire to give more to their children than they had, they should think back to their youth and go deeper than what money provides. If we know as adults what money doesn't buy, then most likely, provision doesn't come from the size and the quantity of possessions. Instead, it comes from the safety the home provides, time with family, vacations, open lines of communication, healthy boundaries, listening, and other relational attributes that invest in the future of all who live in the home. To each their own, but here's what I've learned. I've climbed ladders, made more money, had more responsibilities, and each came at a high exchange rate. Decades from now, what will your children say about their first memory of money, how they were rewarded, encouraged, and the like?

Money — Switching gears back to our exchange rates for international travels, be aware of the rate at which the currency you are most familiar with is being converted. In many cases, an exchange of currency is not required while crossing borders; however, the cost of goods and services will be different. This is nothing new to the well-versed traveler; however, you should be aware that customs and traditions also vary; leaning into the differences and similarities is a great learning tool. In doing so, we just might learn to appreciate more of what we and others have.

Equally important, if you choose to live in different countries for extended periods such as in retirement, be sure you understand the intricacies of exchange rates and how they will change the amount of money that will cross borders. For example, if someone sells stock in one country to transfer cash for income into another, taxes in the country of origin will often apply, and exchange rates come into play. Depending on the direction one chooses to move money, that could make a considerable difference.

Leadership
We should be asking and listening to our team's life balance needs and also learn from these exchanges. For example, how has the hybrid work environment promoted productivity? Did this come at the exchange of another KPI?

Are your leading indicators tracked? If so, what is being exchanged for them? Also, how are your trailing indicators tracking on this exchange? Do some team members feel like their exchange is different than others? Remember, that proximity still matters for a large percentage of the workforce.

Life

For the qualitative aspects of life, exchange rates can take on a more favorable appearance—one that doesn't show one side getting a better exchange. Think ying-yang and a great partnership. Think of both sides of a coin, both different in appearance; yet sharing a story for the country of origin while also providing value in the form of currency. Think of mutual understanding and respect.

Wealth Coordinate: When we take care of ourselves, our amazing body and mind are equipped to return the exchange. Both are far more resilient than we give them credit, and hopefully we can all agree that our bodies are incredible works of art amazingly equipped to do phenomenal things. In this relationship, we can seek an exchange that produces mutually beneficial outcomes beyond our best dreams. To this end, it's helpful to review our own deficits and in doing so increase our wealth. For the most part, this is within our control much like your exchange with your employer. What is your health exchange? How do you speak to yourself? How is the way you speak to yourself affecting the physical exchange? Remember we are incredible works of art amazingly equipped to do phenomenal things; oftentimes, the difference between those who succeed and those who don't is the belief in themselves.

In our most trusted and valued relationships, including with ourselves, similarities and differences exist, and it's the coupling of these that deepens and broadens the strengths pool. And just like you might see or accept risk differently than your spouse, best friend, or business partner, it's likely that you also have different reward systems, love languages, and biases. Plus, I can say with almost 99 percent certainty that you have different upbringings. To know your upbringing, biases, experiences, successes, failures, and the like is to accept the makeup of other valued and trusted relationships. It is in this mutual, healthy exchange that we are more apt to live an abundant life while also being better equipped to tackle the storms of life. Why? Because stuff happens. To trust this process, we should also accept that others are better than us at certain things and that's exactly why we should lean into these relationships. Furthermore, you also have strengths that should be shared in a healthy manner. It's in this mutual exchange environment that weaknesses get covered by strengths. Let's get out of the kiddy pool.

Finally, here's why money will never buy love, joy, peace, and the other best things in life: Money is transactional; it is an exchange. For your work, you get paid. To buy food, you give a portion of your income to someone else. If you barter, you give someone something for something else. But the best things in life aren't transactional. We can enjoy the qualitative and seek the quantitative. We can be more interested in how we feel and look rather than basing our happiness on a number on a scale. We can keep our gaze on the people we're with and enjoy proximity, or we can be lured away by a screen. We can focus our efforts on gaining more stuff while missing out on what we value most. I'm pretty sure that at the end of my life, the hours I worked, points I accumulated, and other counted stuff will not be what I'm most thankful for. Or should I say, at least I hope so?

Let the haters hate. Debt instruments like anger, bitterness, immaturity, and the like are far heavier than pounds, more blinding than poor eyesight, and more crippling than a torn Achilles.

Risk

There are numerous risks related to investing and the growth of assets. Here's a list of several risk factors, which we will unpack without industry jargon:

- **Market Risk:** Markets move up and down by the second; this risk reminds us that investments can decrease in value.
- **Political and Geopolitical Risk:** Do we need any help understanding that politicians can create issues? I didn't think so, but just in case you do, this risk reminds us that domestic and global political issues can increase the potential for loss in investments.
- **Inflation Risk:** Think back to our earlier discussion of inflation. This risk reminds us that costs will increase over time.
- **Longevity Risk:** Simply put, this refers to the risk of outliving your money.
- **Concentration Risk:** Remember the collapse of Enron? This risk speaks to the importance of spreading out investment dollars rather than investing large percentages into one stock position.

- **Horizon Risk:** To understand this risk, think about the investment advice someone who is retired would likely give to a young family. Most likely, their desired outcomes are different. The young family wants to grow their investments over the next thirty-five years, but the retiree is seeking income from their investments now.
- **FOMO (Fear of Missing Out):** The fear of missing out on a good thing. I think we all know what that feels like.
- **"Knee-Jerk" Risk:** I think many of us have experience with this risk; it speaks to the lack of perspective and reacting without insight.
- **Yolo:** This isn't the acronym "You Only Live Once" mantra of adolescents but rather, it refers to a life not lived on purpose and the risks associated with the ill-prepared.

Risk takes on various forms and is more often present than not. It can positively or negatively affect our short- and long-term outcomes. It can tear down walls and build them. It can increase values and diminish them. It can create opportunities and squander them.

Wealth Coordinate: To know how risk can inform, prevent, and provide is important to our personal and professional lives as well as our investment portfolios.

Risk is everywhere and always present. Some of it is within our control, but most of it is not. Feel better yet?

I remember seeing a rope swing for the first time as a kid. I was less willing than others to risk what I thought was life and limb until I did, and then you couldn't keep me out of the rotation as we climbed the tree, took the leap, swung out over the water, let go, flew for moment, and swam back to shore.

When my parents dropped me off at my college dorm, I remember thinking, "What am I doing? I know one person on this campus; I'm a social guy and not a great student." That lasted until I met a dude wearing a South Padre T-shirt from Channel View; then Brandon and I became best friends, right out the gate.

I remember moving to Chicago after graduating and hearing most of my friends say, "You're crazy. Why would you leave Texas!?" I knew I could always move back if it didn't work out, and trying something new while someone was paying me sounded like an opportunity. Isn't it interesting that when we speak of risk, we often fear the loss while not evaluating the potential reward.

Application

Here are a few helpful thoughts pertaining to risk related to investing.

- Diversification in investing is very important. Think back to our review of the various forms of risk and the adage of "don't put all your eggs in one basket." Kinda makes sense after seeing how one investment can fluctuate or decrease drastically. That is why in most cases, investing should include a broad range of investments, aka a portfolio.
- *Risk Tolerance* is a term used in my professional world daily. Here's the issue with terminology used in my industry. Who talks like this? Most of us while hanging out at the water fountain, watering hole, dinner with family, hanging with friends, church, or kids' activities don't say to someone, "Say, how tolerant are you of the risk related to your daughter's learning time horizon?" So, here's the takeaway, risk is inherent with investing.

    Accounts will fluctuate, sometimes more than others. They will go down in some years, but are they trending up and to the right over time, and if so, are they trending at a pace that you are comfortable with? That's your risk tolerance, how comfortable are you with your account losing value during market volatility? But remember, managing risk is learned much like my rope swing story and better understood over time just as trust is built in our most valued relationships. It takes time to know and understand how tolerant you are with how the markets work. To get punch drunk after a great year of returns is as risky as running for the hills after a year of poor returns. Just like the lane you prefer on the highway, know the lane you prefer and if you choose to change, use your blinker, look over both shoulders (briefly), check your mirrors, and then move over if the lane is clear (metaphorically referring to your approval).

- When will you use the money? Sounds simple, I think. My industry uses time horizon to ask the same question. Again, this is not language that is relational. Here are practical examples of the time horizon concept: When do you think you'll need money to pay for your child's college? Or when do you think you'd like to retire? There you have it—a simple and easy conversation-starter. Here's a helpful way to see how these terms fit within these examples. Time horizon is the number of years before money is needed for a specific purpose, whether near term or way down the road. This intel then helps determine how the portfolio should be built.

When it comes to understanding the risks in investing, remember that the risks cannot be removed. There is risk in burying it or using a coffee can, and there is risk in buying publicly traded investments. There is also something to be said about research, due diligence, and working with professionals. And, of course, there is also risk in working with someone who is a self-proclaimed anything. Did they give themselves the title of expert, business coach, specialist, or was that term given by the industry that they earn a living in, with credentials, and licensing, and experience and clients.

Life Application

What does your personal portfolio look like? If you were to create a pie chart and allocate the importance of what matters to you most in life, what would it look like? Leave the percentages out for now. Here's mine:

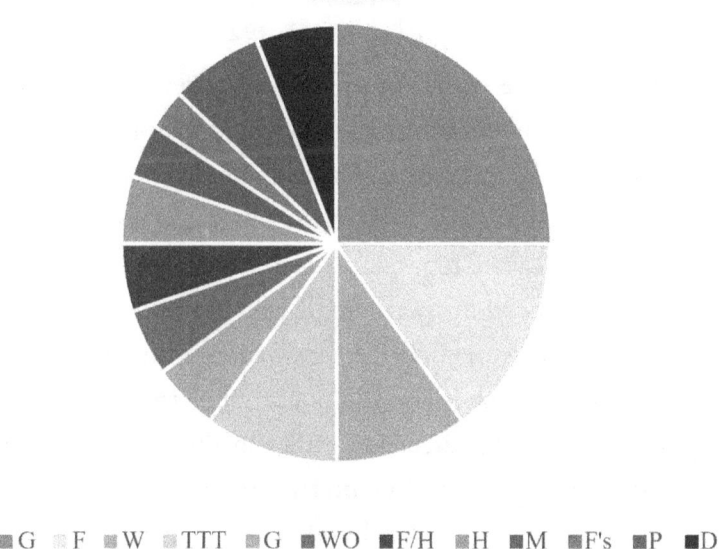

■G ■F ■W ■TTT ■G ■WO ■F/H ■H ■M ■F's ■P ■D

Our personal life portfolio allows us to look at the opportunities as well as the potential loss that risk introduces. Here are some of the categories I choose to invest in my personal portfolio:
- **Spiritual Health:** My highest priority in life is my spiritual health, and there was a time in my life when I served at church too much. I tell you that not to boast but to serve as a warning to those who don't know when to say no. I signed up

for almost everything the church requested and was gifted with several amazing experiences. I also learned the hard way that serving, for extended periods of time, shouldn't come at the sacrifice of family and my own health. There will always be a need, and I can't fill all of them. I'm grateful that I learned about balance and the risks associated with service.

- **Family:** I love my family, and I recognize that I am blessed to say so. I'm thankful that I get to spend time with my family, and I'm also thankful that I can give them what my parents provided for me. The risk of not leveraging the time we have is as detrimental as missing out on the Eighth Wonder, compounding.
- **Career:** One of the easier risks to review is our work. For starters, I should say that I truly enjoy what I do and that I'm fortunate in this regard. However, there are risks I must pay attention to such as working too much and doing the work of others. If I work too much, I sacrifice family, health, rest, and all three are in my portfolio. If I do the work of others, I run the risk of preventing their growth and diluting the group's potential, which is also in my portfolio. This harkens back to the life-balance discussion earlier in this chapter. Life is full of balancing acts and by understanding the balance, I create more potential. Conversely, if I do not understand the balance, I run the risk of losing some or even all my personal portfolio.
- **Health:** I'm appreciative of my ability to enjoy golf, work out, and do other outdoor activities. If I fail to prioritize my physical and mental health, I'm agreeing to diminish my ability to enjoy these things that charge my batteries; that would be a big risk to me. Plus, each of these activities takes time, energy, and money, and we know if we exceed our margin in this area, we risk developing an unhealthy

relationship with these gifts. On the positive side, when I prioritize my investment in each activity, my batteries get charged, I stay healthier, and I experience more of life. That's a lot of upside potential.

- **Growth/Development:** I enjoy growth, learning, stretching my abilities, testing my strengths, and seeing results. When I play golf, I want to better my score. When I compete, I like to win. At work, value and speed are important KPIs for me. There's nothing wrong with any of these, until there is. When winning becomes more important than those I enjoy being with, I run the risk of losing relationships. When knowledge becomes judgment or a holier-than-thou mindset, I run the risk of isolation. When I don't appreciate others on my team, I run the risk of lowering team morale. Conversely, when I take risks to be vulnerable and transparent and trust others to do their part, the team has a higher probability of success.

- **Money:** We all need money. We are all consumers; there are things we need, things we want, and things we wish to have. If we know the balance of our income and the 5Us of money (i.e., giving, saving, spending, debt, and taxes), we are more apt to live in alignment with our values and seek a higher quality of life. If we don't know our balance, we run the risk of living out over our skis or worse yest, pursuing someone else's lifestyle.

- **Friends:** You might think this one is self-explanatory, but it's not, and it's hard. A healthy mix of friendships brings life, and an unhealthy mix has the potential to bring ruin. The risk of not appreciating those in your circle comes at a cost as life's demands create friction and present inconveniences. However, isolation has its own risks as does not making changes in our friendship circle when needed.

As you can see, there are numerous risks associated with our personal portfolios. Remember that although risks come with potential losses, they also bring potential gains. And both will vary in value. Take this simple but common example for a spin. If I run the risk of discomfort by telling a friend that their zipper is down, I forfeit a little embarrassment to help someone else potentially avoid a greater embarrassment. In exchange for my brief discomfort, I gain appreciation and respect. How much different is this from seeking help from a professional?

Let's use a fable of "The Scorpion and Frog" to illustrate:

> A scorpion is sitting on the bank of a river and needs to cross but it can't swim. It sees a frog on the other side of the river and asks the frog to carry it on its back across the water. The two have an exchange starting with the frog who hesitates and says, "You'll sting me!" The scorpion then says, "No, I wouldn't do that because if I did, we'll both drown." So, the frog, convinced by the words of its enemy, agrees to help, swims across, and allows the scorpion to catch a ride.
>
> Halfway across the river, the scorpion stings the frog. "Why did you do that?" exclaims the frog. "I couldn't help it," says the scorpion. "It's in my nature."

It's in my nature . . . As I see it, this fable is not only about the scorpion; the frog plays a key role in this fable. Like the frog, each of us has the opportunity to take on upside risks that benefit ourselves and others.

- Do you know what's in your nature?
- Do you know what parts of you resonate with the frog of this fable?

- Do you know your strengths, desire to help, and your willingness to go out of your way for others and for yourself?
- Do you know your motivation to take risks and make sacrifices for others and yourself?
- Do you know your blind sides that persuade you to take risks that maybe you shouldn't?

Think about your personal portfolio and consider creating a resource that is easy to reference. You can create a pie graph that lists your strengths from highest to lowest, assigning a percentage that each has in your strength pool. You can also take this a step further at work and share your portfolio with your peers and direct reports. If you'd like to improve your quarterly or annual reviews, review the exchange rates of strengths and outcomes. For example, here is my strengths chart:

Professional Strengths

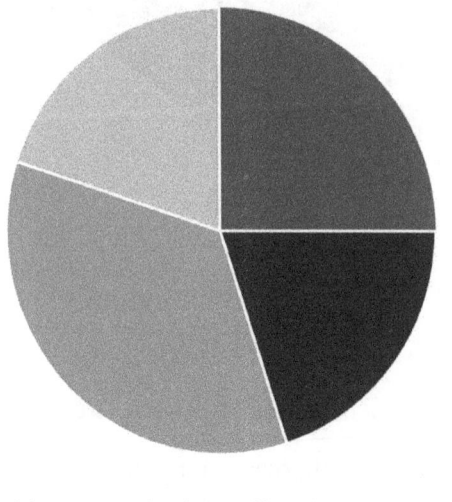

■ Creativity ■ Team Oriented ■ Problem Solver ■ Positive Nature

I chose various colors of green to symbolize strengths because we must talk about the outcome of this timeless story. As the fable goes, after the scorpion stings the frog and excuses its action with "it's in my nature," they both drown.

Each of us has characteristics that are like the scorpion. We all have our issues, our hang-ups, fears, and insecurities. No one is perfect and, therefore, we can drag ourselves and others down with us. However, we also have the option to be more like the person we aspire to be. Not like the frog, but better.

We'll talk about this in a minute. To review one side of the coin is to admit there's another side. You can't eat a slice of ham without biting both sides. Even if it's in a wrap, both are bitten. So, here's the same illustration but with weaknesses.

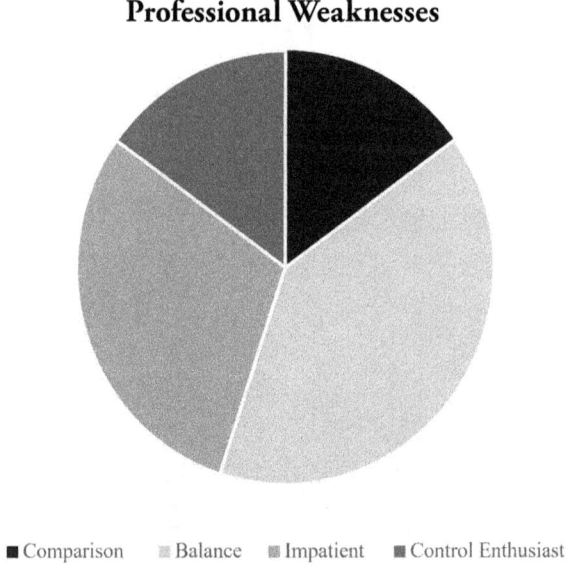

■ Comparison   ■ Balance   ■ Impatient   ■ Control Enthusiast

By understanding our own strengths and weaknesses, we gain insight into an important part of our make-up or environmental DNA as I call it. In doing so, we learn to invest in ourselves rather than attempting to change others first.

It is difficult to love and lead ourselves simultaneously and without comparison. It is in this sweet spot of self-assessment, however, that we can both lead and love ourselves well. In turn, we pave the way toward a brighter version of ourselves and a better tomorrow.

To help, let's lean on the importance of diversification. In a well-constructed investment portfolio, various investments are chosen to work with each other in various market conditions. They're not designed to respond to volatility the same way simultaneously, and they are not asked to perform equally. Much like the snowshoe distributes weight, making it easier to walk across the snow, diversification is intended to help us weather difficult seasons and capitalize on good seasons.

How well are your personal, professional, and investment portfolios diversified? What are the known upside and downside risks.

- Our thought patterns: We've unpacked this numerous times, and this fable speaks to the importance of our thought life. Know your strengths and weaknesses and how your thought life revolves around them. What upside risk have you experienced? And don't forget about the other side of the coin. How much downside risk have you experienced because of your thought life? Are your thoughts aligned with your risk tolerance?
- Trusted advisors matter: We've unpacked this too. Know who you can call at any given time and who will listen and help.
- Know where your wisdom comes from: I can't emphasize enough the importance of seeking wisdom often. Wise counsel can come in various forms and from a variety of people. Seeking wisdom can also help avoid larger issues. Remembering that with the two sides of every dollar, you may be able to provide insight into opportunities that others may not see.

- Know your growth trends: If it's valuable to you, it's worth tracking. You might find that you're in a sweet spot of measurable risk and outcome. That's a healthy place to be.
- Know how lifestyle creep sneaks into your life: We talked about this in the chapter on inflation. Much like wrinkles can slowly make their way into our appearance, so can debt instruments like self-doubt, perfectionism, greed, and dozens more. These can hide away and be costly to your bottom line.
- Know how you are consistently investing in what matters most to you and learn how to starve what you don't want. Our minds work like our physical body in this regard. Invest in what you aspire to be while monitoring your intake in all forms.

Also know that for every strength, there is an excessive side that can cause a strength to become a weakness. I learned this moons ago. I was taking an assessment, which confirmed some of the strengths I already knew about myself. The same assessment spoke of the misuses, excessiveness, and downside risk when strengths were pushed too far. That assessment had more of an impact on me in exposing my downside risks than my upside potential. Such assessments can lead to a form of diversification, which can be very helpful. In our willingness to shine light into the corners of our mind, we expose blind sides.

Leadership

Taking risks is part of the DNA of business, and many phrases have been coined specifically to express this thought. I'd like to encourage all leaders to better understand the risk of not helping your valued team(s). If a leader is only evaluating strengths and weaknesses, we're missing out on a ton of useful data.

Review the list of risks we started with in this chapter and ask how each plays a role within your team(s). Here are a few examples to help:

- Market Risk: For this I'm reminded of the saying that real estate is worth what someone is willing to pay for it. Some buyers are OK with overpaying, and others always want the "good" deals. How are you investing in your team so that when the market comes to attract your key players, a conversation ensues rather than a two-week notice?
- Horizon Risk: I have two big pet peeves with corporate America that I think fall into this risk category. The first is the thought that executives are capable of choosing mentors for team members that they know nothing about, and the second is the assumption that great sales professionals automatically make great leaders. These poor practices have plagued growth within great teams for decades. This is not to deny that, in some instances, both have worked, but that's not a common occurrence. Name three great athletes who made even better coaches. Cite two instances in your life in which a prearranged relationship developed into something greater. Relationships are far more complicated than this, and you know this because you're an adult and you've been in relationships. If it's more production you seek, maybe it's better to equip the great sales professional with a support team. If you have wise counsel on your team, be more creative and introduce environments of learning and help develop these skills with support and guidance.
- Concentration Risk: Just as having a high concentration of one position in a portfolio can introduce this risk, high concentration of middle management, an overlap in

responsibilities, and top-heavy structures also promote concentration risk in organizations and businesses. We want leaner, wiser, more agile teams, quicker muscle memory, and growth, but we strap business units across the land with slack that doesn't produce the results we seek. Why? That's your role, leaders, clear the lanes.

- Inflation Risk: We know that things change and that this risk is a silent killer of business just as much as it is in retirement. Are risks going unchecked and, therefore, permitting various forms of creep? If the cost of doing business isn't mirroring the gradual increases in cost, then there's a hole in the bucket.
- FOMO: This is real. Do you know that there are valued team members who don't take vacations because of something they fear. Do you know that there are valued team players who won't delegate tasks because some unhealthy relationships aren't being addressed? Do you know the health of your teams and the FOMO that is not being addressed and the productivity that is being lost because of it?

Leadership is a difficult task, and it's not as glorious as it may appear initially. I encourage teams to remember that leaders are often under an immense amount of pressure to produce results. How can you support them and help? How can you help them diversify thoughts and plans? How can you help avoid "knee-jerk" reactions? Life, career, sport, community—all of these are team efforts.

Investing
I'd be remiss if I didn't come full circle and speak to the importance of understanding risk in investing. There are volumes of books,

articles, podcasts, papers, and events that speak of investing. Here are some additional things to be aware of:

- Start early and know your benchmarks: Several helpful metrics support longevity in fiscal matters. For example, save 10 percent early, consistently keep your debt-to-income ratio in check, and set aside cash reserves. Know what works best for you and invest in something rather than nothing.
- Steady wins more than reactionary: Avoid knee-jerk reactions driven by emotions, impulse buys, FOMO, grocery shopping when hungry, and the get-rich-quick schemes that exist around us. Fueling your strengths and delegating your weaknesses can help you avoid known pitfalls while also creating higher trajectories. Know what you are good at and seek assistance with the rest. There is no shame in this game!
- Risks vary by type and by season: Knowing the purpose of your money and when it's going to be needed helps you establish a proper risk level. Know that your risk level may be different from that of your neighbors, coworkers, and parents.
- Diversification is one of the top three components in investing: Having a portfolio all in stocks doesn't concern me for the higher risk-tolerant investor, but being in one sector or greater than 10 percent in one position should be reviewed.
- Know the purpose of your income: Too often incomes are dispersed without direction. Knowing how your income falls within the 5Us will bring clarity. Knowing what you value most in life and how your income is supporting that will bring self-worth. Solving for tier-2 objectives that support your values and quality of life brings a sense of energy that is hard to dissuade.

Risk is everywhere and will always exist in our lives. It's unavoidable. But there is a ton of joy, rest, peace, and life in understanding and managing the upside potential of risk. Oddly enough, trying to eliminate risk introduces risk. One could argue that the biggest risk in life is not taking any risk.

Net Worth

Net worth is often referred to as a financial equation. Simply said, one's net worth equals their assets minus liabilities.

Assets − liabilities = net worth

But what is an asset? An asset is something that has value or brings value. For example, in financial services-speak, an asset may look like an investment account(s), home, real estate, or intangible items such as patents and royalties. However, your salary is not an asset but an obligation to pay. A liability is a debt that is outstanding and, therefore, owed to a lender or creditor.

One of the flaws in the traditional definition of *net worth* is that it fails to acknowledge that you yourself are an asset, and I submit that you are your best asset. Better said, no matter what your net worth is numerically, your self-worth is far more valuable. And if you have one or more of the following, your total net worth just increased: health, gifts, strengths, personality traits, spouse, children, family, friends, trusted relationships, and career.

So, how do we measure something that is important to us? Remember, if it's valuable, it is worth measuring. Although this chapter focuses on net worth, remember that the discussion about measurement isn't for comparison or bragging or lording over others; it's for growth purposes. If something is valuable, we don't want it to lose value over time. So, we need to ask ourselves, how are we investing in it, and how are we seeing it grow? That's why we measure.

Your worth is far greater than any amount that follows a dollar sign. In fact, your worth should never be determined by any scale or number. No matter the numeric value of your assets, your value as a person is far greater.

Is the traditional definition of net worth helpful? Yes, to some extent; however, it should be factored in as part of a bigger equation. Before we continue, let's look at two examples of a traditional net worth calculation:

- Example 1: Financial accounts (two 401ks) amount to $500K and liabilities amount to $150K. Let's presume the $150K liability, aka debt, is a mortgage and that the home value is $300K. This brings the net worth to $650K. Here's the math:
  » Home value is $300K – mortgage owed of $150K = $150k in equity
  » Total Financial assets of $500k + $300k = $800K
  » Assets of $800K – Liabilities of $150K = $650K
    - From a monetary perspective, the mortgage liability decreases the net worth.
    - For the home, as the home value increases and the mortgage is paid down, equity increases. **Note:** Home values are not guaranteed to increase. I recognize that since 2020 things have changed, but things tend to revert to the mean.
    - The same applies to the financial accounts. As contributions are made to these accounts and as

they grow over time, the account values increase the overall net worth. The same growth principle applies with our account values. As they fluctuate, so does the net worth.
- Example 2: Financial accounts (two 401ks) amount to $50K and liabilities amount to $400K. Let's presume the mix of debt is a $300K mortgage, $50K in vehicle loans, $35K in credit card debt, and $15K in student loans. The home is valued at $350K. This brings the net worth to $0. Here's the math:
  » Home value is $350K – mortgage of $300K = $50K in equity
  » Financial assets amount to: $50K + $350K = $400K
  » Assets of $400K – debt of $400K = $0
    - The liabilities decrease the total net worth to $0.
    - The same growth potential applies to this scenario, yet the debt load is creating drag on the total net worth.

Both scenarios are common, and both have important data points to learn from. Let's review the data:
- Income: In each scenario, the household income is going toward four of the 5Us: savings, spending, debt, and taxes. Let's go back to the income statement made earlier and remember that the income we earn is not an asset; think of it more as a promissory note.
  » Asset: Valuable property or account owned by a person or company.
    - Promissory note: Written promise to pay a stated amount to a specific person at a specified date.
- Financial accounts: Both scenarios have investment accounts.
- Debt: Both scenarios have debt.

- Equity: Both scenarios have developed some equity in their home.
- Net Worth: Both scenarios have a potential net worth:
  » Example 1 has a positive net worth and a quicker earning potential.
  » Example 2 has a debt hurdle to overcome before creating a positive net worth.

Take a moment to do a quick assessment of your net worth:

Assets :	Assets :
Financial accounts = $	Mortgage amount = $
Cash = $	Vehicle loan/s = $
Value in your home = $	Student loans = $
Value in real estate = $	Credit card debt = $
Other, royalties, gold, etc. = $	Other debt = $
Total assets = $	Total debt = $

Total assets = $ _____ – Total debt $ _____ = Net worth $ _____

Note a few key takeaways from this exercise:
- Planning is not utilized as frequently as it could because of the lack of direction, experience, and know-how. These are valid reasons, but knowledge is all around us, and it is incumbent upon us to make time to improve our lives. Planning is a building process, and each step along the way improves upon the previous.
- Debt tends to linger; it does not just disappear. In fact, it will increase if not resolved as the obligation to the lender increases with interest.
- Your net worth exercise can help you visualize where your household income is being used.

Before we move on, it is important to drop a **Wealth Coordinate** here and assess the current environment. Why? Because we cannot determine how to get where we want to go if we don't know where we are.

Where we are in life is a reality. No overtly optimistic or pessimistic view should deter us from the truth. Our income is our income. The amount we owe others is the amount we owe. Our financial net worth is our financial net worth and no one else's. Our wealth instruments are our wealth instruments as are our debt instruments. This is exactly what we need to know before we determine a path for our future.

Here is another truth: No matter the amount next to the dollar sign, your net worth is far greater than that amount. Let's build and review your Household Inventory (HHI) to learn more.

Use as much time as you need to fill in as much as you can in each of the following categories. I suggest that you write as you go and don't hesitate to go to the next category even if you feel you haven't finished the prior one. Go all the way through the categories and then go back and fill in more information as you see fit. The more personal you make the list the better. For example, if you are married, write your spouse's name; if you have children, list their names rather than "children." For accounts write the name such as 401(k), and if the amount is known, provide that too. Don't forget about the things we sometimes take for granted such as freedom and other valuable aspects of life.

Family: _____

Relationships (valued friends, peers, etc.): _____

Physical Property (Real, Other): _____

THE TWO SIDES OF EVERY DOLLAR

Physical (health, strength, etc.): _____

_____

Mental (IQ, memory, fortitude, etc.): _____

_____

Emotional (health, EQ, etc.): _____

Monetary/accounts (name not values): _____

Work: _____

Treasures: _____

Possessions: _____

Talents: _____

Intangibles (time, freedom, etc.): _____

Things passed down: _____

Misc: _____

How did that exercise make you feel?

When I first thought of this exercise and completed it myself, I felt a sense of guilt because "first world problems" can sometimes rob me of the truth. Then, the more I reflected on things given, learned, seen, done, felt, earned, and things I had failed or succeeded at, I realized they have led me to where I am now. With that perspective, my posture changed.

I began to appreciate the collective outcome on a larger scale. Yes, I wish I had done some things differently and yes, I could have made healthier decisions; however, those poor decisions and consequences are now part of my story. I can choose to allow them to help me improve my future or allow them to imprison me. No thanks on the jail time.

Maybe your experience was different, or possibly it was similar to mine. Either way, this is one of my favorite exercises for a couple of reasons. First, it's quite common to go through this exercise and then go back and add more. That's good because as we observe, hopefully we lean more toward thankfulness and in so doing, we learn to appreciate all that we have, and our posture changes. Second, and this is key, after we take an inventory of all that we have and all that we are as a person, then we can apply other insights to help us see why holistic planning is valuable. For example, let's go back to the net worth equation and make a slight tweak.

We know that assets minus liabilities equals net worth. I'd submit that all the items you listed in your HHI are assets. Now let's flip one of your assets, for example work, and ask whether we are allowing our work to transition from being an asset to a liability in our family life.

I fell victim to this in my previous career as my responsibilities pulled me further and further away from my desire to be a better husband and dad. I allowed my salary, bonus structure, responsibilities, title, benefits, and travel to distract me from two of my most precious gifts, my marriage and our daughter. So that equation looked like:

Matt's HHI – work = decreasing value as a husband and dad

The important lesson to take away from this is awareness that our assets, gifts, resources, and strengths can become liabilities. In this equation, I permitted my competitive nature, my drive, and what I thought was the right career path to distract me from my most important roles of being a husband and a dad. I allowed the gift of my career and work to become a liability. In so doing, I created my own deficit in key areas of my life. This wasn't another person's doing, it was my doing, and I allowed it to occur.

Make no mistake, I am not implying that hard work or striving toward a brighter career is a problem. I don't believe that. What I am saying is that you would do well to be aware of the frequency in which work begins to overtake aspects that are more important to you. If work promotes missing birthdays, anniversaries, family time, health or other top-tier aspects of life, take note. Trust me, it can become a problem.

Reflect on your HHI and review all the gifts, strengths, talents, experiences, people, and intangibles you have. If you did not complete your HHI, please stop reading and complete the HHI exercise now. Generally speaking, quick fixes are not sustainable. Another way of saying this is "Band-Aids" don't solve problems; they provide temporary relief for a problem that still exists.

Understanding your full net worth is important as we remind ourselves that wealth comes in a variety of forms. This exercise is helpful because it provides insight into both the things we value from a quality perspective (qualitative) and the things we value that are measurable (quantitative). To understand our full potential, we need to know and grow our wealth quotient (WQ).

Wealth Quotient

You are valuable to all the spheres of influence in which you live and work. You bring worth in many ways—from the gifts and talents that you have to the experiences that you have lived, from the education that you have assembled to the hard knocks that you have gathered from the bumps and bruises of life.

You may already know that your very being is valuable. If so, that is wonderful. If you have not been told this before or if you are unaware of this, please receive it: You are valuable in your home, community, family, friendships, and work environment. Please do not simply read that statement and rush on. Receive this and believe it to be a truth statement. Receive it as if I were giving you a hundred-dollar bill. You'd snatch that hundo from my palm as quickly as you could, and I want you to do the same with this statement about your true value.

It is also important to accept the fact that there are others within each of the spheres in which we live and work who are equally, less, or more talented, gifted, experienced, and knowledgeable. Be encouraged, not discouraged, by this. I urge you to embrace the thought of abundance versus scarcity for several reasons. First, because it is true; just as there will always be those who are younger, the same age, or older than you, the same is true of how we are uniquely gifted with our own set of talents, experiences, education, trials, successes, failures, and so on. Second, when we embrace this view, we open doors to all types of learning experiences.

When we see that there are people all around us who can enrich our lives and vice versa, the concept of high tides raising all ships is realized. I liken this to the concepts of lift and buoyancy. When we accept that "we are fortunate to live and work around others" who are intelligent, gifted, experienced, and talented, the "air" at that altitude is less polluted with negative thought patterns.

The Wealth Quotient consists of six key components: acceptance, evaluation, holistic, balance, preparedness, and communication.

Acceptance
The people we surround ourselves with mold and shape us, and this can either be helpful or not so helpful. The beauty of acceptance is that when we permit others in our lives who are more equipped, knowledgeable, caring, and so on, the better we can become. Because

we all face struggles and strife, we cannot prepare or begin to solve problems with the same mindset that created the problems we live with. As I've stated before, self-help is a fallacy. Be careful with the "I got myself in this, and I will get myself out of this" mindset. At the core of that thought process are many debt-related obstacles. You have people all around you ready, willing, and able to help, and you will be able to come alongside others and help them too.

Accepting the fact that others can help you and that you can be helpful to others is a key component to growing your WQ.

Evaluation

This one can become tricky. Some people find it hard to look at themselves in the "mirror," but for others, it's a breeze. If we accept that there is no perfect person, then we can accept that we have aspects of our lives that are on track and others that need improvement.

What is the shortest distance between point A and point B? Answer: A straight line.

Without point A, what is the shortest distance to point B? Answer: The distance is unknown.

Comfort is a relative state, and I understand that there are varying degrees of comfort. There are also varying degrees of pain. Perhaps if we were more comfortable taking small steps toward some best practices, we might avoid some painful circumstances.

Holistic, Rounded, or Complete

Whichever best fits your eye and ear, "holistic," "rounded," and "complete" are synonyms. The thought is to include all aspects.

The traditional net worth formula we walked through earlier is a quantitative exercise. It measures the numbers but does not consider the qualitative wealth components listed in your HHI. Your total net worth is comprised of all that you offer and all that you are as a person.

Net worth does not boil down to a formula on a spreadsheet. You have intrinsic value that is immeasurable, which means that it is sometimes hard to identify and measure. However, simply because it's hard to measure does not mean it does not exist. Much like in business, some may use terms like *fixed cost, hard cost, soft cost,* or *hidden cost*; either way these terms reflect cost and, therefore, should be monitored.

The total value of your life and the impact you have on others in all the spheres you inhabit will never be fully measured in your lifetime. It's too difficult to understand the impact we have on others and then their impact in their spheres. You are resourceful, creative, and gifted; you are far more important to the bigger picture than even you may see. Thank you in advance for all the value you will bring over your lifetime and that you will pass down.

Soap box moment please: I am not a fan of the term *human resources* in referring to our valued team members. I understand that changing the term will create additional work, but we can't fear work or change. If employers seek more productive work from employees and employees want to be treated in a manner that makes them feel appreciated, then shifts are needed. If you are an owner, manager, or leader of an organization consider the other resources your business consumes daily to produce the products or services that your clients purchase. These resources play a key role; however, whether they are renewable or natural, we are consuming them to produce a product or provide a service.

Do you want your valued team members to feel as if their sole purpose is to be used up? To be seen as a resource is to imply that the employer and employee are in a transactional relationship and that the owner of that relationship is the employer. No doubt the term *human resources* was originally considered to be creative and helpful; however, given our collective intelligence, I believe we can improve this terminology. Let's grow our collective vernacular, be more creative, and refer to our teams in a more meaningful manner. Thank you for that moment. I have stepped off my soap box. Back to our wealth quotient discussion.

Balance

Let's go back to the net worth equation to speak more of the balance between assets and liabilities. From the original exercise, we know that assets minus liabilities equals net worth. I believe that most, if not all, the items you listed in your HHI are assets, gifts, and talents and that they bring value to your life. There are key aspects to these valuable components that we should address—the first being the gift itself and the second being the equity we own.

Let's use the home example from the net worth exercise to speak about both the gift and equity. If you own a home, I hope you listed it as a gift in your HHI. Our homes should also be part of our net worth equation because as we pay down the mortgage, our equity builds. Therefore, the less debt we owe, the higher our net worth becomes.

The same concept applies to all the tangible possessions we own. What's more, the same concept also applies to all the intangible assets we own. For example, did you list love, peace, rest, grace, hope, forgiveness, tolerance, or any other intangible gifts you own? If not, please pause and think through this and add any that come to mind. The intangible gifts we intentionally invest in increase in value and grow in equity over time. Use the examples above as proof of concept.

If you want to understand forgiveness, it will require experience in forgiving others and seeking forgiveness. If you desire rest, it will require more than buying a high-end mattress. If mercy and grace are not present in your life, they will require practice. To love others, you must love who you are and trust your worth. There are numerous examples such as these, and simply knowing the definition of these treasured gifts is not enough. Much like an investment portfolio works best with ongoing contributions and management, our most treasured intangible wealth attributes work the same way.

Preparedness

Preparedness means that you should know what you own and plan what you know. In following this mantra, we discover what is and is not bringing value to our lives. This is why we measure what we value. From there, we invest in our wealth instruments and divest our debt instruments. Much like when your equity in your home improves or when your personal debt-to-equity ratio improves, you are the primary beneficiary of this blessing. That then naturally spills over into other spheres in which you are a beneficiary.

Have you heard of debt-to-equity ratio? From a business perspective, it looks like this: A business produces a product or provides a service and in exchange, it is earning revenue. From the revenue, the business is expected to make a profit. Because of this, it is essential to know how much of the business is operating off borrowed money (debt) versus operating on its own equity (something it already owns). Sound familiar?

It should, as this is very similar to how most homes operate. One key difference is that most businesses keep a watchful eye on the books. Another key differentiator is that great businesses plan by knowing their value proposition, knowing how they differentiate themselves and by producing a valuable product or service. Knowing how we are being leveraged by our debt instruments is as important to us as it is to a savvy business owner. Why? Because the more equity you own, the less someone else owns a portion of what is yours.

Franklin D. Roosevelt is quoted as saying, "courage is not the absence of fear, but rather the assessment that something else is more important than fear."[9] Assess (know) what you own and plan what you know.

Communication

Up to this point, the word *communication* has been used over twenty times. We know it's important, useful, life-giving and beneficial to our 4Ps, marriage, children, family, friends, career, ourselves, investments, and everything else.

The level you invest in your strengths and gifts is proportional to the equity that you have in each. This is very similar to the way you grow financial equity in your home. For example, you can invest in the proper use of your imagination by increasing valuable intangible assets such as courage, hope, trust, and others, or you can allow fear, doubt, worry, and other debt-related instruments to influence our imagination and decrease your WQ.

We must also pay close attention to the drift or creep we allow in our gifts. Reflecting again on my story as I permitted my gifts to drift toward liabilities in my first career. Finally, it is equally important that you identify and address your weaknesses. We all have them. So, who do you trust to help keep them at bay, and how are you helping others do the same? Some aspects of our lives are not gifts but are responsibilities or positions that we have taken on when we could have— and probably should have—said no. Or maybe that's just me.

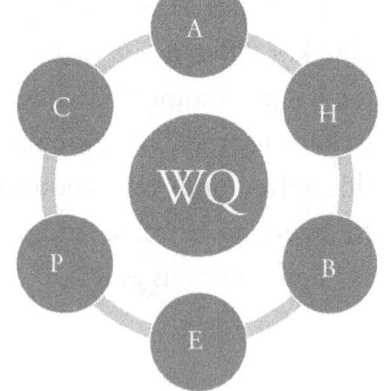

Planning should include the creation of guardrails to prevent us from drifting out of our lanes. If we do not put up guardrails, a gift can become a liability as responsibilities begin to drown out our gifts, or we veer off course. Knowing your WQ will be beneficial to your everyday life. Furthermore, knowing your WQ and planning what you know will change lives, starting with yours.

Application

Know Your Motives

Ask yourself what your motives are. In making tough decisions, determining change, deciphering your plans, and not doing certain things, it is critical that you know what's driving your decisions and actions. Cooler heads prevail for a reason, not by coincidence.

What about when you feel wronged and someone has hurt you, or when decisions you've made create difficult circumstances? I remember being told, "Hey, Son, I know this hurts, but you're going to have many best friends, trust me" or "Son, I know it's hard to make heads or tails of this, but trust us, you will look back on this and see the good that comes from it." I also remember being told, "Son, this hurts me more than it hurts you." Our closest relationships are going to hurt at times. Also, it is important to note that our closest relationships are with imperfect people, ourselves included. Our motives will help determine the recovery efforts and speed.

While attempting to control our motives, remember that we cannot control other people's motives. Nor should we try. If you want to live a busy, nonproductive, hectic life and not find rest, try controlling other people's motives and try believing that you know how others think. Remember, you are uniquely you, and so is everyone else. You might share some similarities with those closest to you; however, you are not them, and they are not you. Having the ability to predict actions within a decent percentage is not knowing how or why someone thinks the way they do.

Years ago, I remember trying to help a friend through some difficult times and he said, "I'm not you, Matt!" Have you ever had someone respond with that truth statement? Truer words have never been spoken. Sorry, brother, I wish I had been mature enough to listen better when I was younger.

Truth and love are two sides of the same coin. But without demonstrating love to others, the truth will fall on deaf ears. Life is best lived with others whose motive is to love you as you are. It helps to know that there are three camps that live around this thought: those who seek growth, those who do not, and those who wait for growth to happen. All of us live in one of those three camps at one time or the other, and we may visit them from time to time. Logic says that each camp will come into play in certain seasons life.

Who do you have in your life that has the autonomy to look you in the eye and speak the truth in love? Do you speak with yourself in truth and love? Seek such people . . . find them . . . a wide range of wealth lives there.

If you are always right or always the truth provider in your relationships, be mindful of that data point as this may be an indication of something that requires attention. When situations arise, it is helpful to have a go-to action. Try asking yourself, "What is my motive in this"? Be honest with yourself as you respond. Ask is my motive to:

- Protect, prevent, bring resolution, or bring peace?
- Seek the bigger picture?
- Control, persuade, or to have my way?
- Avoid issues by being passive?

After you identify your motive, evaluate the effort required to carry it out. Ask yourself whether that motive is best and then adjust if needed. If you really want to double the double and see a productive outcome, share your motives with others, such as your inner circle and trusted advisors. Be transparent and vulnerable when confronting issues. Ask others about their motives while sharing yours. Collect your knowledge and insights; this is good data to keep. If you are entertaining a new working or personal relationship, find out right away whether this is a relationship you want to be in, a business you want to pursue, or a responsibility you want to take on. Along the way, be sure to put guardrails in place.

Is this uncomfortable? Sure it is! That is until you see it work. Are those who lack a trusting spirit going to struggle with this? Yes. That is, until they see how quickly it helps. Are others going to be uncomfortable with the questions and ill-prepared to answer at times? Yes. That is, until they hear your motive and are comforted with your words. Is it possible that alignment does not exist? Yes. And if that is the case, you just saved time, some emotions, and other valuable attributes by discovering this early on.

Your bottom line is your end result, good, bad, or indifferent. It is worth knowing what you are seeking as well as what others are seeking or expecting. Your personal P&L (Profit & Loss) statement should always boil down to more than numbers. More on this later.

Another valuable question to ask is this: What hills are worth dying on? An exhausting life is the life that is trying to fight every battle. You've heard it said that you should choose your battles wisely. Ever heard someone say, "That worked so well we stopped doing it"? We will face thousands of challenges in life, and it isn't wise to fight them all. Know the battles you're willing to stand your ground on and invest in them.

Knowing our motives improves our bottom line, increases our net worth, improves our P&L, and raises our Wealth Quotient. Watch how fast you build your intangible wealth attributes by being aware of your motives and by intentionally investing in the sequence of your thought life. Are you tired of asking, "What keeps you up at night?" Start here and discover how margin feels and how valuable it is to your bottom line. With newfound margin and WQ growth, begin to expand upon your HHI. Journal your efforts and determine what is and is not working. Practice, prepare, and plan your routines.

Share your newfound successes with others and seek to live with an abundance mentality as you seek others who share the same. It is wise to evaluate how your interactions in the past have dictated outcomes and how with a slight tweak, outcomes can differ. The sequence of your thought life matters; your bottom line is a derivative of your thought life.

Leaders, your team wants to be heard. Use these six WQ components during your meetings and reviews. Ask, listen, and repeat. The difference between wealth and health is one letter, and both are dependent upon these components.

Lines of Credit

In the financial world, various forms of credit are available to the consumer. Here are some of the more common lines of credit along with a lay definition of each:
- Personal Line of Credit – borrow the cash, repay with interest, and repeat as needed.
- Home Equity Line of Credit – borrow from one's home equity and repay with interest.
- Business Line of Credit – similar to the personal line of credit but for a business.

These are products on the shelves of lending institutions, but unlike the tangible goods you leave the store with, you leave with a debt obligation. Another product on the shelf and more commonly known, is a credit card. It's essentially the same thing as a personal line of credit.

To help strengthen our knowledge and purpose of reviewing credit, here are the noun and verb definitions of *credit*:
- Noun: (1) the ability to repay based on trust, (2) something added to the sum (subtracts from debits). Both forms of credit are upward, to the right, green and healthy.

- Verb: (1) to acknowledge someone's contribution to something bigger than themselves, (2) to add to an account. Both actions are also upward, to the right, green and healthy.

From these definitions, we're reminded that not all forms of credit pertain to the borrowing or lending of money. Let's unpack that a bit.
- When you think of someone who is credible, who comes to mind? What is it that makes them credible?
- Why are ratings for a restaurant, movie, show, event important? When you check out the ratings, what do you want to know?

Someone who is credible to you is most likely someone who meets one or more of the definitions above. Regarding ratings, they help us quickly evaluate something—either providing credibility or denying credibility.

Consider the lines of credit we have at our disposal in our personal lives:
- Trust – belief in the reliability of someone or something.
- Loyalty – consistent support or allegiance to someone or something.
- Faithfulness – remaining loyal to someone or something.
- Honor – high regard or respect for someone or something; to fulfill or keep an obligation.

What parallels do you find in the lines of credit that can be purchased and the lines of credit we have to extend to ourselves and others?

Because wealth and debt come in various forms, it's important to remember that credit can fall under both headings, and it's our actions that determine which column is supported. Sometimes, emergencies and difficulties arise, making borrowing helpful during those seasons from a financial perspective. However, from the personal perspective, we are not a very forgiving culture; therefore, the use of any personal credit is costly.

My hope in sharing this is to stress that communication is the key to growing the wealth column and limiting the debt column. Let's review some helpful points to consider:

When borrowing money:
- What's the plan?
  - » Reason:
  - » Timeline:
  - » Costs:
  - » Risks:
- Have these considerations been reviewed and discussed?

  If you are not married, consider the benefits of reviewing your plans with someone you trust or someone who has experience with this topic. If you are in a close relationship or married, identify the two things that you both value most and understand how those values align. This step opens the door to reviewing the want or need for taking on debt, and this becomes a good starting point for reviewing the four parts of your debt plan list above.
- Assessment:

  The goal for most of these discussions is to grow our wealth and benefit our beneficiaries. Therefore, it is wise to review the desired outcome, talk about the obligations, and understand the ramifications:
  - » Desired outcome: Who am I truly trying to benefit?
  - » Obligations: What financial and personal costs are related to this decision?
  - » Ramifications: Do the costs pertaining to this decision and the way the decision is being made align with what I value most?

It's amazing what open lines of communication do for our financial and personal lines of credit. This is not to say, we should expect things to always align for ourselves or others. Sometimes, the best decisions don't align with our original thoughts because we discover a better course of action, or a healthy conversation persuades us that the benefits don't outweigh the costs. Either way you win, and that's our Wealth Coordinate for this chapter.

Wealth Coordinate: Open, trusted, and healthy communication benefits you and your beneficiaries, and it is a lynchpin for success.

One last point on credit. If you know your credit score, that's great. If not, request it soon. There are several useful and safe ways to get this helpful piece of data. Here are some helpful tidbits pertaining to our credit:

- Financial credit score: This number estimates the probability that the borrower will repay a debt and pay bills. This is a quantitative measure of historical behavior. These factors determine a credit score:
  » Payment history – on time or not
  » Debt utilization – how much available credit is being used
  » Length of credit history – how long credit has been established
  » Credit mix – mix of credit types (i.e., mortgage, cards, loans, etc.)
  » New credit apps – opening several new accounts within short periods of time
- Children: Age-dependent learning pertaining to financial and personal credit is useful.

Consider resources early on that teach the importance of credibility, character, and trustworthiness. As children age, consider using some metric that helps them see the importance of these qualities and why they matter for adults. When they reach teenage years, consider using age-based credit cards that, with your supervision, help them establish a credit history and begin to understand how the 5Us work. Here are some suggestions:

- » Visuals are helpful: A glass of water can be used to help them see how trust can be added and removed with decisions by adding water or pouring it out. As trust grows, it's reciprocated. Adding a food color has a similar effect.
- » Age-appropriate responsibilities: Help around the house, homework, athletics, the arts, and other activities; most of these have some metric applied to them. For example, first chair in band, first string on the team, and grades on homework—something that helps them see how these apply to life.
- » What I have in mind here is to relate chores around the house to work ethic and show why it matters; relate grades to future income; relate practice to character-building; and relate sharing to team building.
- » This is key to their learning: Keep in mind that they aren't adults yet and, therefore, their learning curve is not your learning curve. Your patience, communication, and EQ are also teaching them something.

- Relational Credit Score: If you think an additional resource might be helpful for marriage or other close relationships, consider using a Relational Credit Score similar to a Credit Score.

THE TWO SIDES OF EVERY DOLLAR

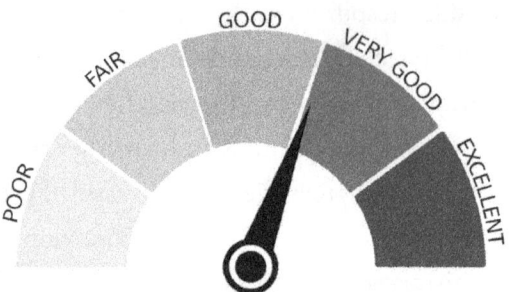

RELATIONAL SCORE

Here are the components of a Relational Score. Talk about the importance of each and determine your own weighted averages:

- **Trust:** for some, trust is earned and for others it's given. Talk about it and where it sits on the weighted scale.
- **Communication:** Communication: for some, open communication builds trust and so communication may be the 35% for that person.
- **Intimacy:** Intimacy comes in various forms and often times one form of intimacy helps with the others. Knowing the differences and the priorities matters.
- **Reciprocity:** mutually benefitting each other is going to provide the best outcome over time. There is a reason why the corded rope is stronger than a single thread.
- **Length of relationship:** it's important for new couples to remember that grace, mercy, and forgiveness are critical at all stages. For couples that have been together a long time it's also very important to remember that opinions, quality of life expectations, values, perspectives and many other important aspects of life will change over time.

Leadership

How are you building credit with your team(s)? What relational equity are you instilling and emphasizing?

As leaders, the sooner we better understand our exchange rates and how those are communicating, the faster we'll see productivity improve. As stated earlier, your team(s) wants to share more. We are no longer living and working in the mode of telling everyone what to do and hovering over them with a heavy hand. Thankfully, we are finally understanding that the individuals who make up our teams are the most valuable aspect of every team. The more and faster we value input, the faster we see a return on investment of time, proximity, energy, and money.

Are there risks? Absolutely. Every relationship comes with inherent risk, but I would argue that the juice is worth the squeeze.

Benchmarks

Have you ever spent time looking at the details and artwork on both sides of either a coin or a dollar bill? For some, it's their passion to know the make and model, and I'm not talking about the differences between a penny and a nickel. They know the years when a nickel was no longer made of silver, the unique markings of each coin, the errors, and how to decipher a dollar bill's potential print flaws. I was in a restaurant recently and when I got my change, I was told that one of my dollar bills had a star next to the serial number. For a second I thought I won a prize. I was then educated as to why the * is there.

Both sides of currency tell a story, and I'm curious to know what a currency that represents your likeness would say about you. Would you use a side or front profile? If so, would it be the more wise or youthful you? Would you edit your portrait beforehand? Maybe you'd add where you were born and what you love. How would you determine the currency amount? What else would you add?

Maybe a better question is, what would you leave out of the artwork? After all, this would be a currency for others to use. So, it's safe to assume that each of our currencies would only show our best sides. Why? Why are we so fearful of our failures? Why are we so concerned about what others think of us? Where did this come from?

With the money in your pocket, can you decide which side of heads or tails you'd like to spend. Can you decipher which side of the dollar bill you'd like to give to the organization of your choosing? Can you determine which side has seen growth and which has experienced loss? Can you determine how many transactions it has been involved in? Can you determine how it has been used in its 5U journey?

No, you can't. Yet it continues to be in circulation, ready for use. It has a purpose, and it is protected by its maker.

As we draw our time together to an end, here is the **Wealth Coordinate** for this chapter: You and I will always have both sides.

We have a left and right side to almost every part of our body, including our brain. We have beauty and pain. Ups and downs. Highs and Lows. Mountaintops and valley floors. Each pair equates to our profits and losses over a lifetime, and I'm here to tell you that your bottom line matters. It's important to you and to your family, friends, peers at work, community, and many others.

If it were up to us, we wouldn't talk about loss; we prefer to talk about profits, gains, pluses, green lines, how great things are, and the like. But that's not always the reality; hopefully, currency reminds us that even though we make mistakes or accounts lose some value or our perceived worth is in question, we still have purpose, and we still bring value.

When conflict arises, the adage about there being two sides of the story is often used, implying there are two different perspectives to one event. Isn't it interesting that with success, we don't say the same? Why is it that failure is what divides, but success is not what unifies.

Let's talk about some widely used practices that are known for improving communication, clarity, and success within the home and business. In the financial world benchmarks, ratios, and other best practices are used to clarify or confirm processes and keep plans on the desired path. For example, a P&L illustrates profits and losses and sums up the two, giving a result, and emergency funds support rainy days while promoting health of an organization.

Several examples can be used to illustrate the importance of best practices. Here's our baker's dozen (B13) starting with the five uses (5Us) of money:

Giving

The most widely known "benchmark" for giving is 10 percent of one's income. Its origin is from the Old Testament and along with the 10 percent guideline, there were several other historical practices used in the Old Testament. The New Testament doesn't specify a percentage; instead, it encourages a person to be a cheerful giver, one who doesn't give reluctantly or under compulsion (2 Corinthians 9:7). The New Testament also emphasizes that giving should be personal and with purpose.

Another helpful thought about giving is captured in the 3Ts of time, talent, and treasure. This useful reminder emphasizes that giving isn't only about money. Using our time, gifts, and strengths to help meet the needs of others is immeasurable and invaluable.

I think that a fourth T should be added—one that might be the overarching T. Any guess? How generous are you with the thousands of thoughts you have daily. What percentage of your thoughts are related to debt instruments? Are those thoughts on autopilot and therefore repeat. It's hard to be generous outwardly or to ourselves when our emotional and mental health is struggling or if past hurts are permitted to linger. Once again, I say, "The sequence of your thought life is critical."

Saving

A common benchmark for savings is 10 to 15 percent of your income. Another helpful benchmark emphasizes the use of one's salary as a multiple for savings. For example, having the equivalent of one's salary saved by the age of thirty and then saving multiples of one's salary as they age. For example, the goal would be to have three times your salary by age forty, six times by age fifty, and so on. This benchmark points out the power of compounding growth and ongoing contributions to investing, which we reviewed earlier.

And much like generosity, we can't decipher which side of the coin does what, but we know we can't give or save what we don't have. This illustrates the importance of the sequence: Investing in what you value most and then paying yourself before spending is ideal.

Spending

Here we are, more than a hundred plus pages in and we finally address one of the elephants in the room. Thousands of suggestions and hundreds of books have been written on budgeting and the like. Instead of repeating what most say you should do, I ask this question: "If you could go back and do this thing called life over, what would you change?"

This is as close to the crystal ball as we can get, and the value of this exercise is a multiplier to your future. We just talked about the thousands of thoughts we spend daily. When you wake up, what's the first thing you do? When you are at a stop light, what are the other drivers looking at? In a restaurant, what are at least half the people doing? Answer: They are looking at their phones and demonstrating nervous energy.

How we spend our days, our thoughts, and the income we earn is worth measuring, and a healthy ratio is one that mirrors what you value most. A part of our spending is required for our needs, and it's also healthy to have wants. In fact, for most households, this is the largest use of the 5Us, and that makes sense. Again, the key is to decipher what sequence you desire most and then align spending with that sequence.

For example, here's a simple percentage of income reference to build upon. Set a goal for the percentage you want going to each category: % toward what you value most, % toward savings, % toward spending (needs and wants). With this outline, you will have a ratio that appeals to your values, future, and current needs and wants.

Debt

There are several benchmarks, ratios, and best practices related to managing debt and as we discussed previously; some debt is seen as advantageous. That said, all debt should be addressed purposefully. Here are some helpful financial benchmarks related to debt in the home:

- Housing Ratio: The financial services industry suggests <28% of gross monthly income should go toward all housing costs (i.e., mortgage, taxes, insurance, and HOA fees).
- Debt to Income Ratio: The financial services industry suggests <36% of gross income should go toward all debts of housing, credit cards, auto loans, student loans, and so on.

This is often referred to as the 28/36 rule and in adding this to the quick reference presented in the "Spending" section, you now have four of the 5Us built.

Taxes

We started this section with giving and finish with taxes. Who said healthy conversations aren't fun? Our taxes vary by household, and different variables determine our annual tax obligation. One of the keys to managing this use of money is to leverage the tax code in alignment with your values and plan. We each live within a tax bracket, so how do you leverage the tax code according to your plans?

- You know what you value most. So how does your strategy of investing in what you value most align with your tax plan?
- You know your savings percentage. So how does that change or benefit your tax obligation now and in the future? Don't forget about the future. Stepping over a dime to save a nickel is a loss.
- Do you like the weather where you live, or would you consider the career potential somewhere else? It's possible that taxes may differ in that city and state. Look into it.
- Property values are part of most tax filings. It's helpful to know how that affects your ratio. It's also important to know what that means before moving, upgrading, or building your forever home.

Most of us don't like addressing things we aren't familiar with, and with taxes, that's the key. Most of us are required to file our taxes, but using tax codes to maximize your plan is not. The benchmark here is knowing the system or working with someone who does. Don't forget that your time is also valuable. If someone else can complete in a few hours what takes you a day, consider the costs.

Emergency Fund Ratio

A common best practice in the financial world is having three to six months of monthly household expenses in cash. Often referred to as a rainy-day fund or break glass account, this cash is set aside, and its purpose is to be available if needed. In theory, this cash may go unused, but when something unexpected shows up, it's next money up.

Much like we discussed in the purpose chapter, every dollar in the 5Us should have its purpose. The purpose of this cash is to be a reserve, and once that amount is established, new funds are repurposed elsewhere.

Credit Score

As we discussed in the previous chapter, your credit score is a quantitative measure of historical behavior. It's beneficial to have a higher score and wise to start building a healthy credit history earlier rather than later. It's also beneficial to know the less obvious credit score markers such as how borrowing more than 50 percent of a credit limit on a card can "ding" your credit score.

Insurance Benchmarks

The range of coverage and product type recommendations for life, disability, and long-term care varies considerably by person. DIME (Debt, Income, Mortgage and Education) is a useful acronym for deciphering coverage amounts for life insurance. The key with protection is to know what coverage is available, to assess the risk (DIME), and purchase coverage that aligns with your plan. That does not mean one should be over-insured. There are also many options related to disability and long-term care coverage. However, it is always wise to understand your family history as well as your current work environment and health. You should also consider the what-ifs of injury and what the need for care might mean to your comprehensive plan. To make an informed decision, you'll need to explore all product options from various providers, the internal costs of products, and commissions for all products.

Return on Investment (ROI) Percentage

We reviewed the importance of knowing investment returns in our discussions of TVM, R72, and the sequence of returns. The most important factors regarding investment returns are risk tolerance, diversification, purpose of the accounts, and alignment with the investment mix. The key here is to make sure your investments are managed according to your wishes and no one else's, not even the wealth manager or company.

Seasonality

The predictable variance that occurs with different seasons of the year affects most, if not all businesses and departments within a business. Factors such as weather, holidays, traditions, and the like all play a role in inventory, cash flows, personnel, revenue, and profitability. Accepting that seasonality exist in business, planning, and life can help avoid knee-jerk reactions associated with common investment themes such as "sell in May and look away." If you know there's a bump in the road ahead because the highway department put a big yellow sign, you're not likely to turn around and take a different direction. You slow down, drive past the bump, and then proceed.

Net Worth

We reviewed the importance of knowing our net worth a couple chapters back. This ratio is the measure of assets to liabilities.

Wealth Quotient

As a reminder, the components of WQ are acceptance, evaluation, holistic, balance, preparedness, and communication. To the degree that these are included in your personal or professional decision-making, improvement follows. If you seek to improve your relationship with the tier 1 and tier 2 things you value most in life, start incorporating these best practices and watch the progress. I encourage you to also track the intel that follows.

Bottom line, Profitability, Profit & Loss Statement

For business, this is the most effective measure of a company's financial and operational health. This is where numbers speak for

BENCHMARKS

the organization's progress or lack thereof. A Profit and Loss (P&L) statement is a financial record of an organization's revenues, costs, and expenses for a specified period. In theory, it looks and acts like a household budget. P&Ls come in a variety of formats. To help our conversation, here's a simple version of a P&L statement.

Household Name

Year: 2025

Income		Total
#1	$ 1,000	
#2	$ 1,000	
Total		$2,000

Generosity		
Organization name	$ 50	
Organization name	$ 50	
Person, family, household	$ 50	
Other	$ 50	
Total		$200

Saving		
Employer Account	$ 150	
After tax account	$ 50	
Cash	$ 10	
HSA	$ 10	
College	$ 10	
Other	$ 4	
Total		$234
Total Investment Amount		$434

Net Operating Income		$1,566

Spend		
Household Needs	$ 300	
Household Wants	$ 200	
Insurance	$ 25	
Legal and professional fees	$ 2	
Repairs and maintenance	$ 40	
Travel	$ 30	
Miscellaneous	$ 20	
Miscellaneous	$ 15	
Miscellaneous	$ 10	
Total		$642

Taxes		
Property	$ 3	
MUD	$ 1	
School	$ 2	
State	$ 1	
Total		$7

Debt		
Mortgage	$ 30	
Vehicle	$ 10	
Vehicle	$ 7	
Credit Card	$ 2	
Other	$ 1	
Total		$50
Total Cost of Living		$699

Discretionary Income Balance		$867

Goals with Discretionary Income		Total
Family Vacation	$ 500	
Home Improvement	$ 100	
Additional Gifting	$ 50	
Additional Saving - Retirement / Rainy Day	$ 150	
Other	$ 67	
Total		$867

Percentage Income of Each Use	
Percentage Generosity	10%
Percentage Saving	12%
Percentage Spend	41%
Percentage Taxes	0.4%
Percentage Debt	3%

Household Triple Bottom Line Use by %	
Values and Quality of Life	21%
Invest in Family (marriage, vaca., home, plans, etc.)	57%
Invest in Future (retirement, college, legacy, etc.)	19%

Publicly traded organizations are required to file a P&L quarterly, and P&Ls are required for tax purposes for sole proprietors and pass-through entities. These statements are useful in the business world for many reasons, and the same is true for the home.

Closing Thoughts

There you have it, your baker's dozen benchmarks, ratios, and best practices for the home. The purpose in sharing these is to shed light on the fact that progress toward what we aspire to most is possible, and we have numerous resources at our fingertips to help. With these lucky thirteen, you don't have to guess or wonder what is going toward what you value most or what is preventing growth or what is left at the end of a season or year.

Imagine knowing how your wealth-driven thoughts are being countered by debt instruments and how each contributed to your daily activities (Net Mental Income).

Imagine applying the seasonality that affects our lives and planning for it better. Again, we've already talked about the top ten list of future planning needs. Imagine knowing how your data feeds your 5Us and how each is working daily toward your future dreams.

Remember that profit is a form of wealth. So, how are you profiting from your wealth instruments, your income, your most valued relationships, your investments and your life? It is not wrong to think or plan this way, especially when profits are reinvested and leveraged well. The possibilities are immeasurable and that's why knowing your data is so important. Be creative with these ratios and benchmarks. For example:

- If your generosity goal is 10 percent, are you generous to yourself? How much forgiveness and grace are you giving for past mistakes?

- If your investing goal is 15 percent, what percentage of your time are you investing in your 4Ps and the top two things you value most?
- We've talked about using the TVM formula and how that applies to several other important aspects of our life. How are those being used?
- For your P&L, you can be creative and connect your HHI with your net income and show how you're investing in everyone in the home. This is also an opportunity to brag about your spouse and children while also speaking life into your family.

These and other creative topics are conversations that can be talked about at family meetings. Healthy businesses aren't just pocketing and spending earned net income. They know their purpose and how it aligns with their 5Us; they have their own version of a net worth statement; they seek growth, pay down debt on purpose, increase cash reserves, invest in teams and culture, purchase market share, and invest in R&D and in several other development qualities.

Our households can operate in a similar fashion. Investing in the "bottom lines" that benefit the home most. In fact, here's another business best practice known as the Triple Bottom Line (TBL) that's even better for the home. A Triple Bottom Line in business helps companies focus on more than profits. It's a comprehensive look at the business's impact on people, planet, and profit. How can the home be more intentional and invest in what it values most? The answer isn't universal; however, you can determine what works best for your home.

- Part of the answer is being prepared for difficult times. Businesses create plans for "what if this happens" or "what if that happens." We used to do the same in talking about fire safety in the home and what to do if someone smells smoke. There is a reason why you touch the door to feel whether it's hot . . .

- Part of the answer, as odd as this may sound to some people, is there's a part of us that understands that it's not all about money. Therefore, if that's all that's talked about, then, people check out.
- Part of the answer also stems from not being able to visualize the entire picture. Hence the crystal ball concept. If we could look into the future and see the outcomes of our actions, most of us would alter our decisions. For the great outcomes, we'd invest, and for the poor outcomes, we'd avoid or choose a different path. The good news for us is that we have the second-best option to the crystal ball, and it's called our past.
- Another part of the answer is that because great businesses know and understand their purpose, they talk about it often. They meet to review progress; they hold each other accountable, prepare, reward, assess risk, and promote change. All on purpose.

Our home life serves a purpose too. Some would argue that its purposes are even greater than the business world. So, how does the home become more intentional? It leverages what is working similar to what we see in the business world, and it tweaks these best practices for its benefit because the environment and needs are different.

Applications

The following graphic shows what a Triple Bottom Line (TBL) for your home could look like:

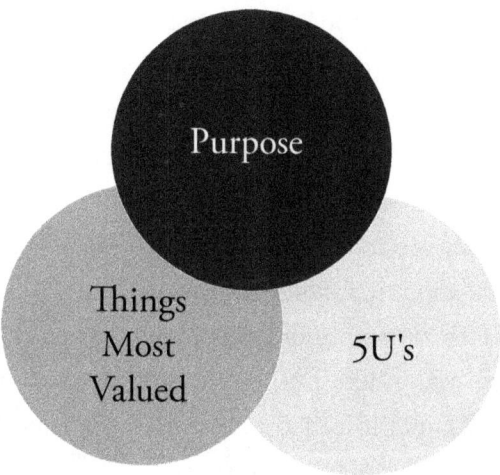

Hopefully, you know your purpose. If so, put it in that circle along with the two things you value most:
- #1
- #2

As well as the tier 2 things that you value:
- #3
- #4
- #5

And, you know your 5Us.

The completed diagram illustrates how your P&L could point to your triple bottom line, speaking life into how the household income is going toward the things that are valued most, how purpose is being fulfilled, and how the 5Us are supporting both.

Congratulations, you now have what most people want: clarity, communication, and progress.

Leadership

What's the TBL you're implementing to lead others well? If your team feels that its purpose is to serve the organization at their expense, that won't yield the highest productivity potential.

It's also important to remember that each person may want their own TBL. Encourage this thought and talk about this more frequently while looking for overlaps. Use synergies to create momentum and differences to build bridges. Use these in your reviews to learn about what hurdles they see and then find ways to move them.

Sometimes, alignment will be difficult. That is, they are not you and vice versa. This is an opportunity to strengthen the relationship, sense of team, and skills. If the lens that is used most is seeing weaknesses and faults in other people first, it's time for some new prescription lenses. Or maybe a mirror.

What would both sides of your currency look like?

Let's Land the Plane

Let's begin our final descent.

I'm hopeful that our time together has proven that much knowledge is available to everyone who wants to know more about investing in accounts and investing in ourselves, our 5Us, our interactions with other people, our conversations, and the way we see the future. There are mountains of useful data for us to know and learn more about. It's also helpful to remember that data is neutral.

Have you ever pondered how everything we do produces a result? Our sleep, eating, drinking, work, and relationship patterns all provide data. Likewise, our parenting, marriage, thoughts, and driving patterns provide data. And thankfully, screen time was recently added to the data list.

And that's ultimately why these topics are helpful. If we say we value "ABC" and "DEF" above all things, how are we making sure that what we value most stays at the top of our priority list? How are we creating guardrails and preventing blind spots. How are we reviewing our tier 2 most valued aspects? How are we preparing for seasons of life that we are excited about? How are we talking about seasons of life that concern us?

Here's part of the difficulty we all face. We live in a low-commitment culture—at a time in our history when our primary form of communication doesn't mean interacting with each other nor does it require a response. This is a time when we're required to have a device that then bids for our attention and opens the world's bidding for the same. We're pursued around every corner by marketing, noise, and fear. We say we're honest and even start sentences with that assertion as in, "to be honest," but are we being honest with ourselves? All this mental stimulation creates decision fatigue and because we live in a low-commitment culture, many important matters are swept under the rug, and others are blamed.

It doesn't have to be this way. Bit by bit and with the help of others, we can review our patterns, learn more about our data, and leverage our own strengths to track toward who and what we aspire to be.

> Again I ask, what is the shortest distance between point A and point B?
> Answer: a straight line.
> Without point A, what is the shortest distance to B?
> Answer: the distance is unknown

The way we invest our income toward the things we value most yields a lot of useful learning experience. The way we function as a fiduciary to ourselves and others yields a lot of useful learning experience. When we look at our personal exchange rates, are we more concerned with increasing our value at the cost of others, or possibly worse, are we lessening our value to be liked? When we consider inflation, do we fear losing ground rather than look for ways to combat it? When we look at how often we're investing in

LET'S LAND THE PLANE

ourselves and our closest relationships, are we tracking upward and to the right? If so, we are engaging in useful learning.

Visibility into our own patterns and behaviors is as unique as our own DNA. When we take an interest in it, trajectories change. Whose, you ask? Remember that both wealth and debt have beneficiaries, starting with us, the owners of our own data. Here's some good news. A lot of this DNA is now available to you via your HHI and net worth statements. We've also talked about things we've learned from our upbringing and experiences. Combine these with the things you value most— your 5Us, and 4Ps —and voila, your DNA strand is now more visible. And your Point A is now defined, allowing you to determine the shortest distance to point B.

As we prepare for landing—we're returning to our seats and putting our tray tables up. Let's remember that it is important to know where we are landing. Let's talk more about where we're headed and how to get to our destination, Point "B," and beyond.

Visualization

In sports there's a concept known as visualization in which you close your eyes and visualize what you expect to happen. For instance, a golfer will stand behind the ball and literally see the shot they'd like to make. The baseball player will visualize the pitch being thrown and hitting the ball with a specific result in mind. The football player will visualize the play unfolding and how they'll perform or react. I once heard Dat Ngyuen talk about how visualization changed his entire football career and how his first football coach would require each position player to lie down on the gymnasium floor and visualize the plays for their next game, both offense and defense. He said that this practice helped him see plays develop sooner, and it "slowed the game down" for him. Obviously, several things worked for Dat at Texas A&M and the Dallas Cowboys. And also in his life.

What's the point with this idea? Herein lies our next **Wealth Coordinate**: This wise exercise is not reserved for the athlete. You and I can do the same for our lives. We can visualize the outcomes that we'd like to experience and how we'd like that to unfold. We can visualize situations and how we will react in preparation for important meetings. Don't forget to invite your team to participate in visualization. We can think through problems in advance and plan how we will react in certain scenarios. And we can plan for the various seasons of life because we have visualized them before they happen. There are no hidden secrets regarding the use of visualization.

We want great marriages, we want our children to launch as successful adults, we want successful careers, we want to enjoy empty nesting, we want to have a seamless transition into retirement, we want to help aging parents and yes, when our time comes, we want to be ready to pass on. All of this is within us to visualize.

Do you know what is similar to visualization? Dreaming about a brighter tomorrow and hoping for something greater are very similar to visualization.

If you are in a great spot now, visualization or dreaming about brighter days may come easier; you would be wise to leverage the time and jot down those ideas. If you're struggling to dream about anything now, know that this is OK. This isn't the pull yourself up by your bootstraps of old and stuff down feelings or past hurts and forget the past. That's temporary learning with massive side effects. As mentioned previously, the bumper sticker is correct when it says that "stuff happens." It's OK to feel stuck. It is important, however, to talk about that with someone.

Please remember the discussions we've had about both sides of the coin; "stuff" can be both difficult and good. It can be awful and great. We wouldn't know what good or great is without struggle. And let's have a truth moment together: If life was all lollipops and ice cream, at some point, we'd complain about the flavors. It's in our nature.

Here are some helpful tips for using visualization:
- Solitude: Find a quite peaceful space.
- Breathing: I've learned a lot from hot yoga; one of my discoveries is how shallow my breathing is.

- Routine: How often are you quieting your mind? Try coupling something you enjoy with a new goal; this is referred to as habit coupling. For example, if you enjoy your morning coffee, try not grabbing your phone for a few minutes. Note that our devices can be added to our list of vices . . .
- Permission: Allow yourself to dream. Permit yourself to look beyond today.
- Journal: Capture what you were thinking and feeling at that time. Look for patterns. There's helpful data to record in your notes.
- Reasoning: As we said earlier, our emotions aren't always our best friends. Apply logic to your thoughts as frequently as possible. You'll know this is being applied when thoughts are not being persuaded by emotions.
- Outcomes: When thinking from point A to point B, be aware of the obstacles, but don't make them your focus. I once played golf with a gentleman I met at the course. He had played there several times, which means he had course knowledge. About the fifth hole I noticed when he talked about the hole, he talked about where not to hit the ball. Not once did he say something like, "See that tree in distance; that's your line." If you visualize what you don't want more often than what you do want, I'm sorry to report that your aim will be off.
- Prepare: It's useful to know what you want but if you're not prepared for it, it could pass you by. Do you know how many famous athletes are now famous because they were prepared when they were called off the bench.
- Be realistic: Dreaming is a wonderful practice that visualizes from point A to point M or beyond, and that's the point. But there are eleven letters between A and M. Your progress depends largely on how realistic you are in the actions you take toward your dream.

Here's the hope with visualization. There are many reasons why thinking about the future isn't considered a best practice. But I believe that the gift of imagination or visualization is available to everyone; it is a best practice for many professionals for great reasons.

Here are some things to consider when visualizing your future, but don't try to visualize all of these at once; that would be difficult, if not impossible. Remember the wisdom we gained from the tortoise and the hare: bit by bit.

- What are your hopes for the two things you value most?
- What are your hopes for your tier 2 values?
- How would you like to spend the time you have with the people you love?
- Who in your spheres of influence are you investing in, and who is investing in you?
- What seasons of life do you want to prepare for?
- What legacy do you want to leave?

Let's keep going.

Family Meetings

Consider the feasibility of routinely scheduled family meetings. If the term *meeting* doesn't land well, change it. Use other terms such as *family conversation, family discussion,* or a combination in conjunction with your last name like, Miller Time. Ha, I bet you didn't see that coming.

The purpose of family meetings is to remove all distractions and hold family conversations. Sometimes, these meetings will be short; other times, they may be hours long as everyone is enjoying the time. When I was growing up, we'd sit around the living room—with Dad on the floor, Mom on the couch, and my sister and I sitting wherever we thought was best at the time. Sometimes, we'd talk and then watch Johnny Carson and laugh together. Other times, more for me than my sister, there were times of correction. A lot of the time, our family conversations were at the dinner table.

Let's recap and remember what you are investing in:
- The top two things you value most
- Marriage, spouse, and self
- Children: their social interactions, problem-solving, communication, eye contact, education, launching, as well as their future adulting, parenting, and someday reciprocating your care for them

- Avoidance of creep
- Legacy
- Communication and proximity
- Future

These are short-, mid-, long-term and generational investment strategies. Scheduling will vary by home, but establishing some routine is best. Determine what works best for your family. More than once a month might be too much, but less than once a quarter is probably not enough.

Ad hoc meetings will be needed periodically. If so avoid using them for only difficult conversations. Another suggestion, if an ad hoc meeting was held between regular scheduled conversations, at your next scheduled conversation, discuss how the ad hoc meeting helped and benefited the whole. Specifics are useful. Share your appreciation for everyone's willingness to gather. If the family is unable to make progress on an issue or if an issue is long term and difficult, find space to share openly.

Each meeting should be a safe and informative time. In choosing topics to discuss, think through what works best for the year that lies ahead and be sure to intertwine the things that you value most. A lot of planning gets derailed as one person's preferences are discussed more than others. Consider using the calendar as an opportunity to talk about what you would like to accomplish throughout the year and add those to future meetings while taking steps toward long-term goals such as college and retirement. Parents, it's very important that you have meetings by yourselves and with your children. Quick side note to parents: As much as you love your children, it's important that you vacation by yourselves too.

Encourage children to prepare for your time together and give them useful examples that benefit their development. For example, if they appreciate more responsibilities, find a way to monetize that with recognition of homework, completion of chores, or the like. If they appreciate time with you, praise, or extra time with friends, look for opportunities to reward them for accomplishing tasks at home and school and talk about those during your time together.

Here's a "macro" model to visualize the year conversationally. As topics such as school, dating, trials, achievements and other important topics are known, insert them as you see fit.

- **January**
  - Conversation about things we value most.
  - Things we accomplished last year as a family.
  - Things we'd like to do this year as a family.
  - Is there anything that anyone wants to talk about?
  - Money topic.
  - Celebrate something.
- **February – Long-Term Goals**
  - Conversation about things we value most.
  - College.
  - Retirement.
  - Are we making progress toward our family goals? Talk about results and rewards.
  - Is there anything that anyone wants to talk about?
  - Celebrate something.
- **March:**
  - Conversation about things we value most.
  - Spring is almost here. Is there something that we'd like to do together?
  - Is there anything that anyone wants to talk about?
  - Do we want to talk about anything that we are struggling with?

Mom and Dad: This is your chance to invest in generational learning. It's OK to talk about life and work trials. It's OK to talk about money and health. And be OK with that fact that your children may not say anything . . . yet.
- » Celebrate something.

- **April**
  - » Conversation about things we value most.
  - » Is there anything that anyone wants to talk about?
  - » Money topic.
  - » Are we making progress toward our family goals?
  - » Talk about results and rewards.
  - » Celebrate something.
- **May**
  - » Conversation about things we value most.
  - » Recognition month: for grades, graduation, work accomplishments, family accomplishments, etc.
  - » Celebration ideas.
  - » Summer plans?
  - » Is there anything that anyone wants to talk about?
  - » Celebrate something.
- **June**
  - » Conversation about things we value most.
  - » Are we making progress toward our family goals?
  - » Talk about results and rewards.
  - » Is there anything that anyone wants to talk about?
  - » Money topic.
  - » Celebrate something.
- **July**
  - » Conversation about things we value most.
  - » Second half of the year check-in: How are we doing?

- » Encourage open conversation. Mom and Dad, silence is useful. Your words are also life and helpful. Remember tone and word choice matters.
- » Is there anything that anyone wants to talk about?
- » Celebrate something.

- **August**
  - » Conversation about things we value most.
  - » Is there anything that anyone wants to talk about?
  - » School, extra-curricular activities, work, age-appropriate discussion.
  - » Money topic.
  - » Celebrate something.

- **September**
  - » Conversation about things we value most.
  - » Is there anything that anyone wants to talk about?
  - » Thoughts about the upcoming holiday season. Talk about vacation time. What would be helpful? Opportunities as a family, gifts lists, etc.
  - » Celebrate something.

- **October**
  - » Conversation about things we value most.
  - » Is there anything that anyone wants to talk about?
  - » Money topic.
  - » Celebrate something.

- **November**
  - » Conversation about things we value most.
  - » What are we thankful for, and what can we do to demonstrate our thankfulness?
  - » Is there anything that anyone wants to talk about?
  - » Celebrate something.

- **December**
  - » Conversation about things we value most.
  - » Celebrate the year, accomplishments, and family.
  - » Family.
  - » Community.
  - » Is there anything that anyone wants to talk about?

With some topics, there will be a tendency for some family members to shy away, and others will want to be the focus. The key is to lean into these moments and ask, "How are we going to accomplish these and grow together?" Some helpful reminders:

- Remember that growth is gradual, and it will take time to learn how to communicate effectively. This is, however, one of the most influential strengths you can bring to the family. Growth and effective communication are generational investments.
- When seeking suggestions, be patient, helpful, and encouraging. Help doesn't imply stating the answers for others, nor does it come from discouraging words.

For meetings with children, introduce age-appropriate learning opportunities. Future colleges and employers will be looking for adults who have several of the qualities that are learned at home: work ethic, integrity, and problem-solving, for example. These qualities won't be taught by future employers; these and other qualities should be instilled before careers begin.

Be creative with their homework, grades, extracurricular activities, chores, teaching them how to treat others and themselves. You've got a ton of useful data to help them learn and grow.

Mom and Dad, use your experiences from work as examples. You know what you dislike and what you appreciate. You know the leaders who are less productive with useful feedback and those that are helpful. You know how you feel about constructive feedback and what you value from your quarterly or annual reviews. This is a wonderful opportunity to create future leaders who believe in themselves and who also appreciate and understand the importance of working with others. This is a life-breathing, career-building, accountability-instructing, family-enriching opportunity.

Be creative with your time and enjoy it with food, conversation, and laughter. Be sure to allow time for everyone to speak and speak up for those who don't. Watch for trends and use this opportunity to talk about how much you love your children and how proud you are of them and how excited you are for their future as well as your future. If you are married, the same goes for your spouse. Children appreciate authenticity and genuineness although they may not articulate this until later in life, but they know these traits when they see them.

Be sure to use specifics when talking about accomplishments. If you have more than one child, be mindful of how you handle rewards; avoid comparison of quantity or quality.

When accountability conversations are needed, no adult appreciates being singled out in front of others at work, and family members are no different. Use one-on-one conversations to address more difficult topics, and be specific. Most of us have felt and dealt with a variety of debt instruments in our life, so be transparent with yourself and your children when dealing with such issues. Issues related to guilt, shame, doubt, and other life struggles are best addressed in safe environments. You'd be amazed how quickly you starve these debt instruments for others and yourself by having open and honest conversations.

Singles and single parents, find others that you can have adult conversations with and use the same conversations to learn more about what others are doing. This may be difficult; however, your 4Ps, the things you value most, and your future are important and worthy investments. Find others to help invest in you and vice versa.

If conversations become emotionally charged, take a break. Remember that it's the relationship that you're fighting for. Once you reconvene, ask permission to talk about what drove emotions one way or the other, before jumping back into the topic. If permission isn't granted, ask if it's permissible to proceed with the same topic or whether it is best to discuss something else. If children were present during that time, talk about it while teaching them that conflict resolution will play an important role in their lives.

Nonetheless, it behooves all interested parties to find the root of the emotion which led to the heated reaction. Something is there, and it would be wise to find a way to talk about it in a healthy manner. If the underlying issue is not talked about, it will eventually come out somehow, somewhere, and the fallout may be far more difficult to work through.

Finally, learning how to own our mistakes and effectively apologize is a generational investment strategy. This is a wealth creation skill set. That is, the various forms of wealth that exist in all of us flourish in healthy soil and being able to apologize, accept forgiveness, and reciprocate these with others creates various forms of wealth. It will also create a living and generational legacy.

In your planning, be sure to talk about the seasons of life that you know are on the horizon. Here's the top ten list that was shared earlier:

- 4Ps: Spiritual, mental, emotional, and physical health. Four gifts to yourself and others.
- Career: It matters to you, so talk about it and plan for it.
- Launching children: Raising and launching successfully.
- Us time: How are you investing in yourselves and your marriage?

- Adult age-based changes: Our bodies, circumstances, and seasons will change. Preparing for these changes is a wise investment of time and proximity.
- Empty nesting: This season is typically considered desirable until it hits home. Things will change and if not talked about, change may be difficult instead of rewarding.
- Aging parents: Some want your undivided attention, and others don't won't to be a burden. Either way, know your plan.
- Retirement and its various components: The transition from work, desired income, longevity, health, hobbies, and activities.
- Life of significance: You worked for decades, now what?
- Death: Hard to talk about, which is an indication of its significance.

For money matters, remember that specificity is aged-based and interest-based. When teaching children:

- Relate to their needs, wants, and ages. Remember that you were their age once.
- Know what they perceive as a reward; it may be completely different from your perception.
- You don't have to know everything. Who does?
- Be open and transparent. How valuable are our failures? If you keep them secret, they have far less value. If shared, the perceived and realized value is potentially immeasurable.
- Earlier is better. Our children are far more resilient than we give them credit for.
- Plant early and often. Talk about high school while they are in middle school and college while they in high school and career while they are in college.
- If you are married, work as a team.

- Body language matters. You see it in them. Trust that they see it in you as well.
- Last and possibly most important: Allow them to be kids; they'll be adults soon enough.

Each of these is a short-, mid-, long-term and generational investment.

As your family matures, conversations will become more complex; then it will be healthy and wise to expand your family conversations with topics such as these:

- Location of estate documents and what to do with them when needed.
- Desired outcomes for things you care about most.
- Legacy plans – hopes for traditions, family history, and generational aspirations.
- Ask if they have questions, and do your best to answer them.
- Long-term care aspirations.
- Provide reassurance that you have plans in place or that you are working toward them.
- Share your desired expectations.

Interest-Based

Although we're all interested in various things, that doesn't mean that we're interested in things that we know are valuable to us or that we'll agree on the topics. For example, our 5Us, investment accounts, and topics related to money are often difficult to talk about at home. Other topics also fall into this category—no need to mention who, but some people don't like going to the doctor or asking for directions, but eventually, they learn that being lost or ill causes setbacks. Here are some helpful thoughts to consider for difficult topics:

- In a marriage, knowing the things you both value the most and then using this information to build common ground is useful. Visualize a drawbridge coming together permitting commuters and commerce to thrive. Without the bridge, jumping from one side to the other like the movies portray is unlikely. But listening and sharing will demonstrate an interest in what each other values.
- Remember the bigger picture and what it is your working toward. Talking about this will help create an opportunity for invest in the future.
- Blended families have some complex matters to work through. Build upon past learning experiences and mistakes you have overcome. Talking about age-based topics, with empathy, will demonstrate an interest in all parties.
- If communication gets "stuck" in a spin cycle, take a break and agree upon a time to reconvene. One person may want to solve the problem quicker than the other person; be aware and remember the bigger picture.
- Knowing who is for you is important to remember. No one will ever agree with themselves on everything in life; add someone else to the mix and the statistics worsen. However, effective communication is possible. Problem-solving is possible. Life is a team event.

On that note, let's talk about planning and how this widely known best practice can be added to every home.

Planning

Living on purpose requires focus, focus requires a plan, and planning requires a process.

Life is a team event. No matter the activity, we are always better when growing and building each other up. Marriage, parenting, work, worship, lifestyle, health, sickness, death—you name it, better outcomes exist for those who tackle life experiences together. While I was talking about some trials recently with a friend, he said he believes, "People are put in our lives for two reasons, blessings and lessons." Thanks, Keith; I appreciate that thought.

Life is sometimes tough, but it is also glorious. Yet our trials, wins, losses, ups, downs, gains, grief, mountaintops, and valley floors provide us with thousands of opportunities and ways to learn.

From my personal life and professional experiences, I believe there are three core components that will help us live on an upward trajectory: (1) knowing your purpose, (2) building your team, and (3) creating your plan. By knowing, having, and implementing these three key aspects in your life, you will live more abundantly and see life from a different perspective. You will avoid simply existing and instead live more vibrantly. In so doing, you will help the next generation. When you experience trials, as we all do, you will be better prepared than not. You will positively influence your sphere of influences and your community. And, when your journey comes to an end, it will be more about the dash rather than the two dates.

Up to this point, we've talked about several aspects of investing that when incorporated into our lives and accounts, will help both. From here, we're going to pivot to planning; to start the discussion, let's learn more about our PTP:

 P = Purpose
 T = Team
 P = Plan

Purpose

We all have a purpose. What's your purpose? Your purpose is as much about attitude as it is ability. You are a gifted person; let's start with that. Everyone is amazingly complex; everyone has gifts and a purpose.

Many people find it difficult to state their purpose because they find it hard to believe they have one. This is often one of the major stumbling blocks to planning, decision-making, and effective communication. You have a purpose, and your life is important.

To help refine your purpose, resist the need for it to be marketable and on a letterhead or billboard. Keep it simple and precise. Trying to wordsmith something that feels like it is going into the Purpose Hall of Fame will likely delay progress. Simple is best. Afterall, if you can't recite it quickly, how can it be your go-to? A lot of organizations fail to do this well.

Why is it important to know your purpose? Instead of wordsmithing something that appeals to emotions, let's talk about outcomes instead. Your purpose is a decision filter. How comforting would it be for you to say no instead of saying yes to everything? Your purpose helps you determine which thoughts to feed and which ones to starve. Your purpose is a compass that provides direction; it is a binding agent; that is, it helps you relate to others and create common ground. Your purpose is the genesis of your mission, and it is uniquely yours.

How reassuring is the thought of having these characteristics built into your life? Does the person you aspire to be have these characteristics?

Knowing your purpose, gifts, strengths, passions, biases, and being familiar with how your experiences have equipped you is a battery charging life exercise. Knowing what tasks you dislike and which to-dos you run toward will complement your daily experience. Growing your awareness of these and how they are being fed will fuel your life. Increasing your knowledge of the data you create and what trends you see in your data will be extremely helpful.

What's your purpose? We'll revisit this question shortly.

Team

Iron sharpens iron. Who is on your team? Who do you listen to the most? Who have you given permission to speak truth into your life? If you are married and your spouse is sitting next to you quickly smile and say, "That's you, honey." Hopefully, that's a truthful answer, and I'd add, other than your spouse, the same question applies. Who can speak truth into your life?

Who has the authority to speak life into your words, thoughts, actions, and decisions? Who is helping map out your plans? Who has your best interest at heart? Are your listening skills engaged? Who brings the best skill sets to the table, and who brings the best out of you? If your team were a sports team, would it be in the playoffs annually? Would it be competing for championships? If you are a Christian, how often do you invite the Trinity into your planning? Who is on your team, and what are their roles and qualifications?

Remember, our closest relationships are among the most impactful strengths and best gifts we have. I'd go so far as to say that relationships, in every aspect of our life, are the key to our collective and individual success. Unfortunately, the people who encourage our growth while sharing the truth in love are sometimes hard to love in return.

When building your team, remember qualifications matter. Do their values align with yours? How do their experiences, abilities, background, and forte align with yours, and do they gel with you? Everyone says they are trustworthy; would you expect them to tell you they aren't? As much as we are alike, our experiences, backgrounds, and training are different.

The lack of experience doesn't define someone, nor does failure. However, we should glean information from others who are able to share applicable knowledge. Why? Because the experiences we have in life will be the lens with which we guide others. Because we have all failed in some aspects of our lives, it is important to take guidance from others who:

- Have experience in working through trials and successes
- Weathered the storms we hope to weather
- Have insights to share
- Are also learning from others

Maybe it's time to start employing best practices rather than common practices.

To see the best return on what this life offers, it is helpful to have a team that knows you and is vested in you and investing in your future. By "investing in your future," I'm not only referring to diversification, risk tolerance, and the time horizons of your investment accounts. I'm referring to planning for your personal and home life, your 4Ps, your marriage, kids, and future. *Wealth management* and *planning* are not synonymous. These are two different skill sets; therefore, your team should be able to speak about each independently.

You might think of your team as your "Knights of the Round Table." Why not have a marriage counselor in your contacts and visit them regularly? Why wait until things are at a tough spot? Why not have an advisor on speed dial—someone with whom you share life events frequently? Why not have the children's counselor in your contacts? Why not include a range of skills on your team, such as a therapist, accountant, attorney, and doctor? It is time for us to stop making important topics taboo and start being more transparent with ourselves and our children regarding these crucial areas of life. It is time to start investing in the most valuable aspects of our lives, not just our investment portfolios. Your team is a key aspect to your life's trajectory.

Who is on your team? We'll come back to this question shortly.

Plan

Where are you headed? I like something Craig Groeschel said at a *Chazown* event I attended in 2012. He said, "Everyone ends up somewhere but rare is the one who ends up somewhere on purpose." That sums it up. Would you prefer to sway with the winds of life and end up wherever life takes you, or would you prefer to head toward a destination intentionally?

Life should include moments of spontaneity, downtime, times with no agenda and seasons of chance. However, when these tactics are the default for setting your direction, they tend to create struggle as time progresses. And, as we saw with compounding growth, it becomes increasingly difficult to make up what wasn't done little by little in the past. No matter the topic, whether it's relationships, money, time, or something else, it is easier to slowly advance toward progress than try to jump to the front.

Are you utilizing your gifts? Are you leveraging your strengths? Please don't view these as a judgment questions. Rather, let's bring some clarity to our collective selves by asking a couple of probing questions: When you picture your best self, who is that person? What characteristics does that person possess? I encourage you to be careful about seeking outcomes that are only geared toward aesthetics or metrics. The adage of keeping up with the Joneses applies to much more than money. Someone else will always have something better, newer, and bigger and if that's your measurement of choice, you will likely be sorely disappointed with the results.

Let's look at the outcomes of having a plan. Some of the outcomes that you should expect from consistent planning include:

- Improved communication, relationships, clarity, transparency, and visibility into important topics.
- More flexibility in reacting to life's various seasons.
- Insight into potential outcomes, goal creation, and completion.
- Alignment with important topics, education, and next generation growth.
- Better mental, emotional, physical, and spiritual health.
- Greater overall preparedness.

As these develop, remember, the sequence of your thought life matters. If we do something so we are liked or accepted by others rather than seeking to help others or improve ourselves, the outcome is a self-fulfilling prophecy. Or better said, only the creator of such goals is pleased or displeased with the results; therefore, the outcome doesn't benefit anyone else.

When you know your PTP, you'll have a go-to for facing life's opportunities, trials, and day-to-day routines. For example, when you're presented with a dilemma, asking, "How does this align with my purpose?" will help your examine your thought process and decide whether to participate.

When faced with a decision about accepting a new responsibility or taking a new opportunity, a review of your plan will help provide guidance. When confronted with conflict or challenging life issues, you will find that consulting with one of your team members may provide just the insight you need.

Opportunities that are presented to us are potentially advantageous; of course, that does not mean we should say yes to every opportunity that comes our way. Some of our trials in life derive from opportunities that we should have passed by. How do you make those decisions? When you are dealing with one of life's storms, a check-in with your team and a review of your plan will help create rational thought and help you avoid knee-jerk behavior. We tend to focus on the dramatic, the mountaintop experience, or the tragedy aka heightened emotions. However, the most frequent type of activity we experience is our day-to-day routines. And, how we develop our abilities for those days matters. A simple analogy helps explain the need.

Think of a profession that is performance-based such as a musician, athlete, public speaker, comedian, you name it. These paid professionals are often practicing, watching film, listening to other paid professionals, receiving instruction, accepting constructive feedback, studying, reading, taking notes, and so on. They do all this so that you and I enjoy their performance. Their day-to-day is no different than yours or mine; it's simply a different profession.

Many of the performances we see are a mountaintop experiences like my memories of Cirque du Soleil. The athleticism, detail, orchestration, speed, music, delivery, and experience of the performers are amazing. We don't pay hard-earned money to see poor performances. We also don't go to see the daily grind of practicing the minor details, blisters, injuries, and mishaps.

Here's a suggestion that connects this analogy to our lives: Start thinking of yourself as a mental athlete or as a small business owner, whichever best fits your train of thought. Both live and breathe in this massive economy known as life on earth. It's helpful to remember that we are not capable of doing everything nor are we capable of being everywhere. Once we recognize and respect this fact, margin in our mind and life improves. Heart rates and breathing slow. No one is capable of knowing all things, being in all places, and expected to have all the right answers. In my experience it's not others who bring these troubling thoughts to our doorstep but rather us who try.

Let's switch gears. In your profession, you are a paid professional, and you bring a lot to the table. Maybe you don't get a medal or get paid like the televised athlete, but that's not the point. When you start believing that you are uniquely talented, gifted, and experienced you will see your life from a different perspective. The sequence of your thought life matters.

We must, however, guard our minds and hearts from becoming addicted to the mountaintops. If we are always seeking peaks while failing to see the beauty in all that lies around us, we miss the bigger portion of what life offers, and we potentially miss out on growth opportunities. Plus, in this world of supplements, we often seek ways to cut corners. Let's be honest. Look at the person who consistently stays healthy, the professional who doesn't job hop, the marriage that grinds life out and you will see a trend. There are very few shortcuts in life. There will always be someone trying to sell you something that boasts of its effectiveness while allowing you to decrease of your time commitment. Simply put, beware and proceed with caution. These tactics act like clickbait and they prey on our minds. Quick fixes rarely work. If they do show results, the outcomes are often short-lived and not sustainable. Yet the industries that focus on pushing quick fix dopamine hits grow richer by the year.

I'll avoid saying there are no effective shortcuts in life because we must be careful with definitive language. Maybe there are a few and even then, those will be specific to each person. I am, however, comfortable saying there are several tried-and-true, non-instant gratification tactics available for our use—one of those being knowing and accepting our life experiences.

Experience is our ally. There's nothing earth-shattering in that statement, but it seems like we are moving away from some proven concepts. Experience is valuable and a trusted team member to our plans.

Mentors, elders, sages, and advisors exist. Wisdom, understanding, and critical thinking are available to everyone. Seek them while leaning into the relationships. Both the knowledge and the relationships are gifts.

Your plan will serve as your own personal navigation system—similar to the navigation app you use while driving. Some people use an app on their daily commute as traffic patterns can vary by the day or departure time. Nowadays, most people use an app while traveling somewhere they haven't been before. The app you prefer for navigation doesn't know the future. Rather it's using data from various sources to help get to our desired destination as safely and quickly as possible. It does this by providing data and helpful information (e.g., notice of a stalled car ahead, accident, toll road, speed, mileage, alternate route); your plan will help provide the same.

And you already have the data . . . None of us knows what tomorrow will hold, and we don't have a crystal ball. That's not planning. However, one way to help "predict" the future is to build the future you desire most. That journey should also have some built-in protection components. That's planning.

Your life is far too valuable to leave to chance. What is your plan? Let's get started. First, let's define your PTP; each element of your PTP should be known, defined, in place and working for you.

Purpose:
- What are your gifts?
- What do you enjoy doing?
- What do you dislike doing?
- What experiences do you have that provide evidence of your giftedness?
- What charges your batteries?

Did you see any trends in your answers? Did this exercise conjure up any emotion toward or away from a particular topic, subject, trial, or accomplishment?

Try writing a rough draft purpose statement. Seek guidance, wisdom, and understanding; exercise good judgment and critical thinking. Planning starts by learning more about your inner self. Use this space to draft some thoughts.

A little trick I like using looks like this. Draw a circle in the middle of the page and write the subject you're brainstorming in the middle of the circle. Then, allow your mind to start doing what it does, think. As thoughts come to mind write them around the circle at the end of the lines. If more lines are needed, add them as you go. It will look something like this:

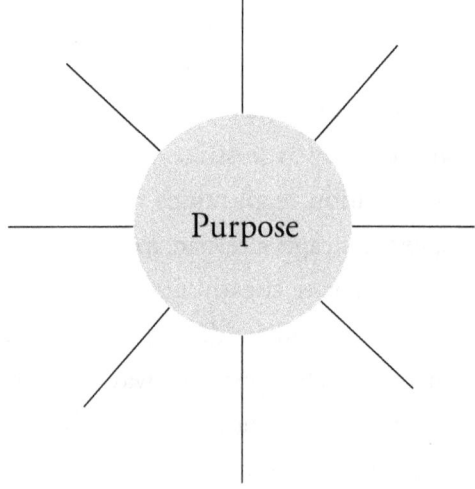

This exercise works well when preparing for other things too. I'll often use this when preparing for meetings or speaking events. I'll follow the same pattern and when the thoughts slow down or I'm done, I'll go back and put a number after each, which then helps me visualize the sequence or order of topics.

When seeking guidance, be inquisitive and ask a lot of questions. It's healthy to know the who, what, when, where, and how. For the Christian, remember that God desires to have a close relationship with you and evidence of this is seen throughout His Word.

Need proof? Jeremiah 29:11 is probably one of the top three Bible verses used to promote planning, but the verses that follow it are rarely mentioned: *"In those days when you pray, I will listen. If you look for me wholeheartedly, you will find me"* (Jeremiah 29:12–13). Also, in the Epistle of James, we learn, *"If you need wisdom, ask our generous God, and he will give it to you. He will not rebuke you for asking"* (James 1:5).

Start small if you run into a mental block; your purpose isn't going anywhere without you. That's the beauty of this process; your purpose is yours and no one else's. Many people have written about how to create a purpose statement. It is helpful to remember that your purpose points to how your talents, gifts, strengths, experiences, and passions align with a grander vision. If you run into writer's block, try removing self from the picture; sometimes, we are the one who slows down the process of formulating our own role.

If you have a spiritual bent, remember that professionals are needed in every arena. By this I mean, being a Christian doesn't mean you must work for a church. The church is about people, not a physical address; therefore, your giftedness can be used in the corporate world too.

I encourage you to develop a purpose that starts within you and develops from the inside out. Whether you believe in God's

Word or not is for you to determine. I submit the following: Debt instruments that diminish the value of others aren't admirable pursuits. For example, neither the unhealthy version of pride nor arrogance is a sustainable leadership quality. I have experienced both of these behaviors from an ownership, subordinate, and inheritance perspective, and I have witnessed the rippling effects of each, by my own doing and by others. My encouragement to everyone is to make your purpose an outward reflection of your inner being.

I truly believe that if we fully understood the impact of creating and including our PTPs we'd run toward a completely different life, a life lived in abundance. I can say this from experience and from witnessing how often we search for answers in various ways. Most commonly, we lean upon a variety of searches and apps as we seek feedback or direction. From search engines to videos, we are often on the hunt for enhancements without a strategy in mind. With your PTP, you'll have a go-to life guide for direction and a resource that is adaptive.

> My Purpose Statement: To worship, disciple, lead, and teach. Something I also know about myself is I'm an experiential and visual learner first.

There are three primary ways we learn. For me, the easiest way to describe these learning styles is captured in the words *seeing, hearing,* and *doing*. My preferred learning sequence is doing, seeing, then hearing. That's why I like analogies, and that's also why I like taking notes and journaling.

What's your preferred learning sequence? What type of environment do you learn the most in, the fastest? What type of environment drags your learning curve downward? For example, learning online and watching videos is not my desired learning environment. I find it hard for me to engage, and it is my inverted yield curve for learning. Instead, I prefer attending and being present. Old school? Maybe. I also like holding a book while reading. This brings to light that not everyone is going to learn as you do. For some, what I just described as my ideal learning environment is laughable. For others, not so much.

Building your purpose will take time; that's all right because you are not trying to wordsmith a marketing plan or mission statement that you are going to hang out front for all to see. Your purpose statement will most likely never be printed on glossy paper and leather bound for presentation. Start small and see how it fits and how it sounds when you read it aloud to yourself. Does it sound like you?

Another benefit of creating and having your purpose is it will help your aim. What are you aiming at daily, monthly, annually? In golf, there's a saying, "Aim small, miss small." From golf to archery, from hunting to basketball, and gardening to hobbies, most activities are aimed at something. Not having an intentional aim for the most important aspects of our lives is costly. It is the equivalent of renting a boat and going out in deep water without any preparation and starting to cast aimlessly. You might get very lucky and stumble upon a school of fish, or maybe you are astute enough to look for the birds and use that as a sign. Then again, deep water is vast, costly—and dangerous at times.

What you are aiming at dictates so many factors, and it complements your purpose. The two work hand in hand and when you have these, your daily activity and routines start making more sense. You start seeing areas in your life that are not complementary to your direction or your purpose.

To understand your purpose, go back and answer the questions above. Look for trends in your writing. What charges your batteries, and what drains them; know what you are passionate about. Be careful not to allow your passions to outpace your purpose. Know your purpose and develop the passions that complement your bigger picture.

Team:
- Personal team members
- Professional team members

Consider these when building your team:
- Be a student first rather than a critic. I believe that people have been divinely put into our life for a reason. Know who is for you and invite them in. Also know that just because someone may appear to be against you doesn't mean they are.
- Whatever prevents you from gleaning advice from others is preventing your personal and professional growth. Abundance doesn't have a scarcity component. Life is way too hard to try to learn everything on our own or critique everyone else. I like the Mickelson mentality. Phil doesn't need to take advice from any player on any tour, but because he is a student of the game, he seeks advice from other tour pros, many younger than he is.
- Your weaknesses are overlapped by someone else's strengths. Leverage this truth at all costs. The opportunity costs lost by not doing so are staggering.

Much of what you have learned over the years has been caught, not taught. Yes, we have learned from books, training, and other designed learning materials; however, we are at our best when in relationships; therefore, we learn while in proximity to others.
- We learn from personal teammates, such as God, spouse, children, siblings, and closest friends. Who is on your team?

- We learn from professional teammates, such as advisors, therapists, CPAs, attorneys, and personal trainers. Who is on your team?

Once you have compiled your team, be sure to let them know. Tell them why you'd like them to be on your team and what you're asking their role to be. Inform them that a plan is coming or that you'd like them to help build it. Also share with them that you want them to play a part in your life and to provide guidance and assistance. If you do this, you will see outcomes you never expected and experience perspective from a completely different altitude. The best athletes and businesses have well-developed teams. Build yours and trust the process.

Plan:
Planning is a well-known best practice and something that is personal to each of us. My hope is that by sharing these topics in the previous chapters, we have created a bridge, a parallel of sorts, between investing in our future and investing in our lives and relationships.

Similar to the habit coupling example provided earlier, when we have topics that we care about that parallel with other aspects that we may be less familiar with, a learning bridge is often constructed. For example, one of my favorite go-to topics in both my personal and professional life is our yield curve conversation. Before reading that chapter, you may not have heard of yield curve or understood what it means in the investment world. However, we've all experienced the negative yield curve of personal downward sloping or accounting "red" days, months, and sometimes years. We know what these times feel like and because of that, we can create a parallel as to what that looks like over long periods. With this knowledge (data), we can better understand why our investments yield lower interest rates because we're less "interested" in having days like those. Conversely, I think we'd all prefer the "normal" upward and to the right "green" yield curve.

In a nutshell, that's what planning is about; it is designed to produce favorable results during "normal," inverted, and flat yield times in life. Its intent is to help visualize what could be and what you want to happen. Planning goes beyond discussions about purpose; it works best when written and readily available.

Although there are hundreds of books on the subject of planning and how to do it well, my encouragement is to create your PTP and start with the following topics:

- Values: What are the two things you value most in life? What are your tier 2 values?
- Quality of Life (QoL): Have you determined the QoL that you'd like to have? Is it aligned with your values? Are your other planning needs supporting what you value most and your QoL?
- Generosity: Your time, talents, treasures, and thoughts are important to you and your plan. How are they being incorporated?
- Cash: It's still a king of sorts; know how much is enough, and how much is too much?
- Savings: Aim small, miss small percentage of income. Know what fits your desired trajectory.
- Investing: Know quantity, quality, and purpose.
- Taxes: they're not going away, but they can be managed.
- Risk: Know the risks your plan is exposed to and create solutions.
- Estate: Know what you want and don't want and get the documents that take care of both.
- Debt: Leverage debt and don't permit it to leverage you.

- College: Invest in the future of children or grandchildren on purpose.
- Retirement: A predictable outcome that you can't borrow for and shouldn't borrow against.
- Legacy: We are all given the opportunity to be remembered for something. This is a choice we get to make.

As you review this list, are there other aspects of your life that could benefit from these planning topics?

Wealth Coordinate: Planning isn't only about money. In my first career I permitted something I enjoyed to overshadow one of the top two values of my life, family. The data was evident and useful in making change. Thankfully, I implemented change and now, in my second career, I get to share that part of my story with you.

With the help of others, I was able to assess the risk and invest differently. I was able to remove the debt instrument of guilt about not being as present for my family as I wanted to be. I was able to improve my QoL and invest in my values. And the list goes on and that's what planning does: It changes trajectories.

So how can you intertwine these planning topics in your marriage, parenting, mentoring, personal growth, career, aging parents, and other conversations? How are these useful in the growth curves you seek?

- For example, insert any of the aforementioned and ask how your _____ aligns with your values and QoL.
- Do you know how it is taxing you spiritually, mentally, emotionally and physically? What risks are you taking or not taking, for that matter?
- How are you investing in your _____?

- Think back to the idea of being our own small business in a massive economy. What are your best attributes, and how are those services being leveraged for your career?
- How are you maximizing your own P&L within your career?

This is why all the planning topics matter. You have it within you to live life abundantly and that doesn't start or end with quantity. It's time to land the plane.

So Now What?

That's up to you.

Hopefully, the time we've spent together has been useful and per the several topics we've reviewed, you see there is a ton of upside available to everyone wanting to invest in their future. Or maybe you feel overwhelmed.

Here is our **Wealth Coordinate** for this chapter and possibly the overarching theme for our time together: The most expensive real estate on the planet is your mind. Why? Because organizations, people, events, and circumstances are constantly bidding for your attention and mining for your data.

Take this as a compliment. Your life, thoughts, and contributions are immeasurable in value. Let's go move some mountains.

To bring our time together to a close, let's talk through some questions. We've talked about a lot and because of that, maybe you feel ready to run through walls, or you may feel overwhelmed. Maybe you're, thinking, "Let's go!" or maybe you're thinking, "What's the point?"

Either way, let's lean upon a basic building block of life and planning using a common phrase known as "crawl, walk, run." This phrase is most often used while emphasizing the need for a process. In reality the process is more like learning to roll over from stomach to back and vice versa, sit up, crawl, walk holding onto a couch, walk, run, and sprint. Learning how to trust a process is already engrained in us. None of us went from birth to the 40-yard dash or learned how to read overnight. Trust the processes that have been proved for centuries:

- You are better equipped to invest in various aspects of your life.
- You are more aware of the benefits related to investing and planning for yourself and what matters most to you.
- You know how important communication is, and you have applicable examples to confirm existing practices or reason to employ others.
- You know more about various forms of wealth and debt and how each affects you and others.

So maybe the "so now what" question is answered best with some follow-up questions:

- What topic resonated with you the most?
  - » Why is this important to you?
  - » Who is involved?
  - » What do you want to invest?
  - » How would you like to proceed?
- For the current planning topics of values to legacy addressed at the end of the previous chapter, which of these needs your attention the most?
  - » Why is this important to you?
  - » Who is involved?
  - » What do you want to invest?
  - » How would you like to proceed?

- Of the planning topics addressed in the Top 10 List ("Value of Your Time" chapter), which one needs your attention the most? If there's more than one, can you prioritize the list?
    » Why is this important to you?
    » Who is involved?
    » What do you want to invest?
    » How would you like to proceed?
- How are you going to invest in your current wealth attributes and the ones you aspire to have?
    » Why is this important to you?
    » Who is involved?
    » What do you want to invest?
    » How would you like to proceed?
- What would you like to do about the debt instruments that exist in or around your life?
    » Why is this important to you?
    » Who is involved?
    » What do you want to invest?
    » How would you like to proceed?
- For your beneficiaries, why are all these decisions important to you?
    » Why is this important to you?
    » Who is involved?
    » What do you want to invest?
    » How would you like to proceed?
- For your 5Us, is there anything you'd like to improve upon?
    » Why is this important to you?
    » Who is involved?
    » What do you want to invest?
    » How would you like to proceed?

Use the brainstorming resource we talked about earlier and note the sequence in which you wish to tackle each subject around the Next Steps visual below. For example, if one of the previous questions resonated with you more than the others, abbreviate it and put it in the twelve o'clock position. This signifies its priority; then, moving clockwise, put the next important abbreviated topic, and so on. If you jotted a note or journaled something from your reading that takes precedent, add that item in the sequence you desire. When you exhaust your brainstorming list, you have a sequence to follow.

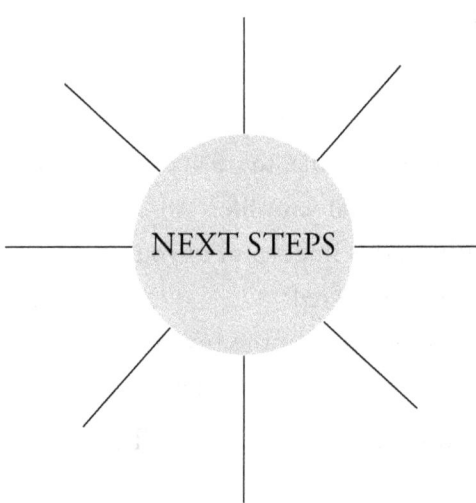

Trust the process. Trying to do too many things at once, no matter how advantageous they are, will create a problem. Home in on the topic that interests you most and begin to unpack the questions provided for each. Lean into what you learned and go back to previous chapters when needed. Trust the process and when you feel you've planned for one topic well, move to the next.

When we invest in ourselves and our learning experience, we will see who is for us, who can help and guide us, who cares for us most, and who strengthens us.

SO NOW WHAT

If you value something, it's worth investing in.
If you value something, it can grow.
If you value something, it can be measured.
If you value something, it should be managed well. If you value something, it should be protected.

Acknowledgments

To my parents, I say, I am blessed. Blessed to have been given enough slack to get in trouble. Blessed to have been loved enough to be disciplined. Blessed to be loved unconditionally. Thank you for laying a sound foundation and for loving me well.

Over the years and in various stages of my life, I have been blessed with many valued friendships, mentors, and leaders who invested in me. To each of them, I express my sincerest appreciation.

To Dr. Caldwell, God bless you. We will see you at some point.

To MM and RR, you know who you are: Thank you. Thanks for teaching a young punk the ropes and caring enough to tell me how things really work.

To my brothers in Houston: I love you. Thanks for speaking truth into me. Thanks for sharing what needs to be heard rather than what I want to hear.

To my daughter: Nothing I can write, say, or do could ever describe the love and appreciation I have for you. You are a gift from God, my treasure in life!

To Leah: Thank you.

To my Savior and Lord Jesus Christ: I've got nothing to bring, and so all I have to offer is a resounding thank you!

XXXXX

NOTES

1. John Rohn, Goodreads, https://www.goodreads.com/quotes/1798-you-are-the-average-of-the-five-people-you-spend.
2. George S. Clason, *The Richest Man in Babylon*, (New York: Penguin Books, 2002), 24.
3. *Merriam-Webster Dictionary*, "fiduciary," accessed April 2025, https://www.merriam-webster.com/dictionary/fiduciary.
4. C. S. Lewis, *Mere Christianity*, (New York: HarperCollins, 2001), 110-111.
5. *Forbes Advisor.* "How to Day Trade." April 16, 2024. https://www.fool.com/investing/how-to-invest/stocks/day-trading/.
6. Sam Swenson, "What Is Day Trading? How Does It Differ from Investing? The Motley Fool, updated September 6, 2024, https://www.fool.com/investing/how-to-invest/stocks/day-trading/.
7. Arnold Schwarzenegger, foreword to *Tools of Titans*, by Tim Ferriss (ebook, 2016), first published on Tim Ferriss's blog November 7, 2016, "I am not a self-made man.
8. *Gallup, State of the American Workplace Report 2019 (Washington,* DC: Gallup, 2019)
9. Franklin D. Roosevelt, Goodreads, accessed June 3, 2025, https://www.goodreads.com/quotes/172689-courage-is-not-the-absence-of-fear-but-rather-the.

About The Author

Growing up in the 1970s on the northwest side of Houston, Texas, I experienced a good mix of city and country living. My introduction to city life was with my single mom living in an apartment in the city. We lived in a square apartment complex with a pool in the center and a "racetrack," aka sidewalk, which allowed easy access from each apartment to the pool and exits to the parking lot. It resembled a courtyard.

I call it a racetrack because I remember my friends and I riding our Big Wheels as fast as we could down the sidewalks. We'd try to do as many three-sixties as we could, by peddling as fast as we could and then pulling the hand brake while cranking the big front wheel to one side. We knew what drifting was before drifting was cool. By the late '70s my mom remarried, and we moved to the outskirts of "H-town" to a small town called Cypress. The big city had not expanded out that far at the time, so there was a sense of separation from densely populated Houston with its big neighborhoods, commercial buildings, and other development. In the southern US, we call this rural living whereas in other parts of the country, this is often referred to as the burbs.

I learned a lot as a kid growing up in Cypress. I was rarely indoors, and my bike was my ticket to exploration until the streetlamps came on at which time, I had best be home. Later, I had a four-wheeler that took me farther than I thought imaginable. Sorry, Mom and Dad, I will tell you more about that later.

I was fortunate to have friends with similar likes. During the summer months, we would be gone all day, and during the school year, only the weather or grounding would keep us indoors. We played football in the street or baseball in the cul-de-sac, and went exploring, biking, and fishing. And later, I even got a Red Rider BB gun.

I learned what boundaries were and why to respect them. I broke rules and felt consequences. I was wrongly accused, rightly accused, punished, and not punished; I was a decent student, decent athlete, and friend. We had rites of passage in which handling greater responsibility led to more freedom or spending money—whether it was timely completion of chores or respecting others or doing first jobs well or, as funny as it may sound, learning how to tie a fishing lure or not running out of gas on the four-wheeler. We did not have cell phones to use when in a bind and we often learned out of necessity.

That was my upbringing; mine was a story with many experiences, which built a solid foundation for what I aspired to be. Learning in our world today is different. When I was growing up, we would joke with our parents because we heard their stories about carrying ice uphill both ways, feeding the animals on the farm, feeding the pets, having one telephone line for the entire street, going from no TV to black and white TV to color TV and then to a TV with a remote, learning how to drive a tractor, milking cows and collecting eggs, working part-time jobs before they were teenagers and full-time jobs when they turned sixteen. We found their stories strange and humorous—from another world altogether. I also remember being corrected with comments like, "Were you raised in a barn?" and "Close the door!" or "We're not air conditioning the outside." and "This [discipline] is gonna hurt me more than you." Most of this is humorous to today's youth.

ABOUT THE AUTHOR

So much has changed. For the first time in the US workforce, we have four generations working together. Or should I say, trying to work together. Four generations represent a wealth of knowledge; the best teams know what they have, and they leverage and deploy the assets needed to accomplish their goals. Yet even though we have this immeasurable talent pool readily available, when we need something, our search for know-how often starts with a search rather than a conversation.

Don't get me wrong; the Internet is helpful, quick, and a great resource that is useful when we want information; it is a game changer in this regard. Ironically, some will read that statement and question the use of the word *game changer* because they grew up with the Internet rather than having to adopt the Internet, which I recently learned is considered being "tech dependent," not necessarily "tech savvy."

Many of our questions can quickly be answered with a quick Internet search. Facts, historical details, recipes, and hundreds of thousands of pieces of information are readily available at our fingertips. However, not all our questions can be answered with this method, and I purposefully use "know-how" rather than knowledge for this reason. Full disclosure: I grew up with shelves of encyclopedias in the living room. I also grew up with what I call the "casket" entertainment system. No joke, the system was about the size of a casket with speakers on both ends that were covered with a burlap-like cloth, and when you raised the lid—that's right, the lid—there was a record player, an 8-track player, and all the storage you would ever need. It was glorious; it was heavy as a house and required a lot of space. I digress . . . thank you.

Today, we find ourselves quickly gleaning information from sources that we don't know, don't know whether we can trust, and don't know what we have in common. Even with people we do know, how many times have you tried the restaurant or watched the movie they recommended and found that you didn't feel the same as they did? Worse yet, when you saw them again, it was awkward, and you hoped they wouldn't ask about the recommendation because that would require you tell them how you truly felt. To avoid confrontation, you might say something that is completely false like, "Yeah, that was pretty good" or "Yes, I thought it was a good movie." Oh how Dr. Phil is laughing right now. I think about his famous line, "How's that working for you?" That is a timeless question. Thanks, Dr. Phil.

Accepting the fact that we're all different is an important component of our lives because we live in a global economy. It is helpful to accept that we all have unique combinations of values, beliefs, experiences, relationships, upbringings, tastes, desires, goals, dreams, fears, doubts, concerns, angst, and other factors that we contend with daily. Funny enough, we keep coming back to the fact that we are all so different yet, we are all so much alike.

My profession is in the financial services industry. Prior to becoming the co-owner of my financial planning firm, I worked in a couple of other industries. My first job was in the packaging industry, predominantly focusing on the agricultural space until I transitioned to packaging primarily for consumer goods. That profession allowed me the privilege of living in several cities. My packaging and business experience then provided the opportunity to transition into the supply chain and procurement solutions field. From there I found my calling in the financial services field. I am a native Texan and a graduate of Texas A&M (class of '95).

www.ingramcontent.com/pod-product-compliance
Lightning Source LLC
Chambersburg PA
CBHW050519170426
43201CB00013B/2016